TOP SECRET

National Security
and the
Right to Know

TOP SECRET

National Security and the Right to Know

Morton H. Halperin
&
Daniel N. Hoffman

NEW REPUBLIC BOOKS
Washington, D.C.

Published in 1977 by New Republic Books
1220 Nineteenth St., N.W., Washington, D.C. 20036

Copyright © 1977 by New Republic Books

Library of Congress Cataloging in Publication Data
Halperin, Morton H.
   Top secret.
   Includes bibliographical references and index.
   1. Government information—United States.
2. Official secrets—United States. I. Hoffman,
Daniel, 1942-   joint author. II. Title.
JK468.S4H34   323.44   77-5349
ISBN 0-915220-27-X
ISBN 0-915220-28-8 pbk.

Trade distribution by Simon and Schuster
A Division of Gulf & Western Corporation
New York, New York 10020
Order No. 0-671-22963-X
Order No. 0-671-22964-8 (pbk)

Printed in the United States of America

Preface

This study of government secrecy was written entirely from the public sources identified in the notes. We conducted no interviews and had no access to documents not generally available. Nonetheless the study was influenced by the involvement of one of the authors in some of the episodes described in this book. The reader is entitled to know of these prior associations.

Morton Halperin had general supervisory responsibility for the production of the Pentagon Papers while he was serving as Deputy Assistant Secretary of Defense 1967-69. He was working on the staff of the National Security Council in 1969 when the United States began bombing Cambodia and was aware of the bombing campaign. The Halperins' home telephone was wiretapped by the FBI on White House orders, ostensibly in search of the source of the leak of the *New York Times* story reporting the bombing of Cambodia. The Halperins have a law suit pending, claiming violation of their constitutional rights as a result of the wiretap. After leaving government service, Mr. Halperin served as a consultant to the defense in the Pentagon Papers criminal trial and as a consultant to the plaintiffs in the *Marchetti* case.

Daniel Hoffman, a political scientist and attorney, has never served in government. He came to this study with an outsider's scholarly perspective, but with a similar conviction that the problem of secrecy cries out for and is susceptible to principled regulation.

This book is in every sense a joint product. We have been through so many drafts and revisions that neither of us can remember very clearly who first drafted which sections. We are jointly responsible for any errors or heresies as well as whatever value the reader may find.

The Twentieth Century Fund provided the support under which most of the research and much of the writing was done. We are grateful for that assistance and regret that it did not prove possible to produce a Twentieth Century Fund study.

Christine Marwick, Florence Oliver, and Penny Bevis bore the brunt of typing and retyping and demonstrated that a stubborn refusal to type what does not make sense can lead to the best and most creative editing.

The election of a President committed to greater openness gives us some added hope that what we have proposed may influence what is done, but we remain convinced that the problems cannot be left to the executive or indeed to the government as a whole. As the Founding Fathers well knew, a people will be only as free and as informed as they are determined to be.

Washington, D.C.   Morton H. Halperin
February 1977   Daniel N. Hoffman

Contents

Chapter 1

Secrecy:
Myth and Reality

Officials are fond of complaining that nothing the American government knows or does can be kept secret. Until recently, most citizens assumed that this was substantially true. On the whole, we did not regret it, for we prided ourselves on the openness of our political process. At the same time, we took it for granted that considerations of national security justify a measure of secrecy in military and diplomatic affairs. This exception to the rule of openness was not controversial so long as the government seemed to apply it judiciously, for the sole purpose of keeping sensitive information out of foreign hands.

Recent events have exploded the myth that virtually nothing is secret. In the aftermath of Vietnam and of Watergate it appears that secrecy has been neither a rare nor a benign phenomenon. On the contrary, the executive branch has made secrecy an essential part of its modus operandi, and the reasons are far more complex than the traditional rationale of national security implies. The Pentagon Papers showed how successive administrations kept Congress and the public in the dark about vital foreign policy decisions. Later, disclosure of the secret bombing of Cambodia dramatized the ease with which even major and protracted operations can be concealed. Congress and members of the public came to feel that they had been systematically excluded from decisions of the utmost importance,

1

decisions in which they had a constitutional right to participate.

Not only has secrecy undermined the constitutional prerogatives of Congress and the electorate, it has also led directly to substantial infringements of civil liberties. The Nixonian passion for secrecy was a prominent theme in the Watergate story, as officials, newsmen, and others suspected of unauthorized disclosures were subjected to such unorthodox and drastic measures as warrantless surveillance, criminal indictment, or court injunctions in restraint of speech. The attempt to justify these measures by the invocation of "national security" has not met with congressional, judicial, or public approval. Instead, there have been vigorous, widespread demands for changes in the secrecy system.

Those who used to maintain that the government has no secrets continue to resist these calls for reform. The abuses of the recent past, they contended after Watergate, were the work of a handful of individuals mostly departed from the scene. Only after the secret intervention in Angola was revealed was there some indication that the "lessons of Vietnam" were perhaps not fully assimilated after all.

Nevertheless, opponents of reform point out, these abuses did come to light. Tampering with the system, they argue, is therefore unnecessary and would only endanger the national security. Indeed, executive branch officials have even revived the lament that nothing can be kept secret and have called for measures to tighten and reinforce the secrecy system.

When, for example, outgoing CIA Director George Bush emerged from a meeting with President-elect Jimmy Carter in Plains, Georgia, reporters asked if they had discussed Mr. Carter's campaign pledge to reduce secrecy. "No," replied Mr. Bush, "we discussed the need for more secrecy."

This incident epitomizes the current clash of perspectives on national security secrecy. President-elect Carter's campaign emphasis on openness in government reflected the public's widespread belief that our worship of the god of secrecy has led us astray. We permitted our constitutional system of checks and balances to be eroded, our civil liberties to be infringed, because we believed that secrecy was necessary to our national security. Now, many outside the bureaucracy have come to recognize that secrecy, far from enhancing our security, made possible the debacles of Southeast Asia, Chile, and Angola. Many have come to believe that secrecy was used to enhance presidential and bureaucratic power and to avoid public debate, rather than to shield information from foreign adversaries.

If these lessons are now widely accepted in the country at large, the executive branch bureaucracy has drawn very different conclusions. George Bush's comment was not meant in jest. Without a doubt, he told the President-elect that we had gone much too far in making information public. Intelligence professionals generally maintain that covert operations must again become the secret preserve of a few within the intelligence community, that sources and methods should not be discussed in public or even with Congress. If the President-elect had conferred on the secrecy issue with career foreign service officers or generals and admirals, he would have been told the same thing. Foreign and defense policy cannot be conducted in a fishbowl, they would say. Too much has been made public; ways must be found to stop leaks and to restrict public debate on sensitive matters.

Congress has for several years been weighing the public demand for more information against the executive branch assertion that if Congress wants access to intelligence it must be prepared to keep the information secret. It has found itself in a difficult position, productive of ironic results. The House Intelligence Committee set up to investigate secret intelligence agency abuses gave the President a veto over the release of information. When the committee, shocked by what it learned, sought to publish its report, the House voted to suppress the paper and investigated its unauthorized publication by the *Village Voice*. The parallel Senate investigating committee uncovered CIA activities, threatening to academic freedom, being carried out on college campuses. The committee report called upon the universities to cleanse themselves, but the committee bowed to CIA pressure and refused to make public what the CIA is actually doing in academe. Now the permanent Senate committee on intelligence shows signs of being coopted into the system. Its members, becoming acclimated to secret briefings, have adopted stringent secrecy rules and begun to talk of the burden of knowing secret information.

As with other aspects of the intelligence scandals, despite the widespread talk of the need for legislation to reform the secrecy system, no bills have been passed.

No doubt Congress hopes that action by the President will solve the problem. But however one assesses the attitude of the Carter administration, history teaches that we cannot rely simply on the good will of the President and his principal advisers. Lyndon Johnson and Gerald Ford, to name just two, came into office committed to a more open system but ended up leading the nation into foreign adventures, vetoing or threatening to veto antisecrecy legislation, and condemning leaks of information they sought to keep secret. The temptations toward secrecy are very great. Information is power; its premature release can kill a desired initiative or lead to severe political embarrassment. It is all too easy for a President to come to the conclusion that he is the best judge of what should be made public.

Moreover, the White House, whatever its intentions, controls only a small portion of the flow of information to the public. Day-to-day decisions made at all levels of the bureaucracy have an enormous cumulative impact. Nor will the bureaucracy be moved by presidential exhortation or executive order. The problem is fundamental and structural. If we are to have less secrecy we need to change the rules of the game, to take away from Presidents and bureaucrats the unfettered authority that they now have to determine what should be kept secret in the interests of national security. We need, in short, laws that will require more disclosure and greater respect for First Amendment values.

In this book we not only argue the case for a more open system, which some readers may find obvious, but we also spell out in detail the kind of legislation we think will in fact lead to less secrecy.

We begin with three stories—the Pentagon Papers, the bombing of Cambodia, and the secret intervention in Angola—that illustrate how the secrecy system works. They are also important parts of the process by which we came to understand the price of secrecy and the need for change.

Chapter 2

Lessons of the Past: The Secrecy System in Operation

Three episodes have had a major impact on congressional and public perceptions of the secrecy issue. Indeed, a large part of the recent and continuing impetus for reform of that system has grown out of the disclosure of abuses in those cases—the Pentagon Papers, the secret bombing of Cambodia in 1969-70, and the secret American intervention in Angola in 1975.

No events in American history have focused more attention on the questions of the government's right to keep information secret, the press's right to publish it, and the public's right to know than those surrounding the Pentagon Papers.

For many, that episode created a new awareness of the abuses to which secrecy is prone. The papers themselves documented persistent and unwarranted deception of Congress and the public. The White House response to their publication brought home the fact that enforcement of secrecy can have a grave impact on civil liberties.[1]

From the start the production of the Pentagon Papers was extraordinary. Early in 1967 Secretary of Defense Robert S. McNamara, unhappy about American policy in Vietnam and frustrated by his inability to change its direction, sought deeper understanding of the problem in an examination of its origins. After consultation with John McNaughton, Assistant Secretary of Defense for International Security Affairs and McNamara's key Vietnam

5

aide, it was decided to set up a task force within the immediate office of the Secretary of Defense. Its instructions were to produce an "encyclopedic and objective" history of the war. The task force was further enjoined to maintain strictest secrecy, not only about the substance of the study but about its own existence. Those recruited were not permitted to reveal what they were working on and no outsiders were to be interviewed. Researchers were to work from documents available in the office of the Secretary of Defense and such documents as they could negotiate, without compromising the secrecy of the study, from other departments of the government, including the State Department and the CIA.

Although McNamara never made explicit his motives for keeping the existence of the task force secret, those working on it lived in fear that an angry President might suddenly order the work terminated and all copies destroyed. Commissioned by an ambivalent Secretary of Defense and produced by relatively dovish officials from the Office of International Security Affairs, the study could only be viewed with great suspicion by the President and his advisers, who were determined to hold fast to the policy in which they had so heavily invested.

As the work went forward, the original intention to finish the work within a few months was abandoned, and a comprehensive history of American involvement in Vietnam was projected, with the deadline for completion constantly postponed. Eventually, the study ran to forty-five volumes and took over eighteen months to complete. Some ten person-years of toil were invested by the task force, headed by Leslie H. Gelb, a Harvard-trained political scientist who had recently joined the Office of International Security Affairs and who worked under the nominal supervision of Deputy Assistant Secretary of Defense Morton H. Halperin. The staff included some thirty-six members recruited from government, the military, and think tanks. Among them was Daniel Ellsberg, a Harvard-trained economist who had worked in the Defense Department, in the American embassy in Saigon, and at the Rand Corporation. Ellsberg helped to draft the portion of the study dealing with the Kennedy administration and contributed comments on the volumes dealing with 1965-66 as well.

As the first volumes were completed, Gelb, in consultation with his superiors, decided that the entire study, page by page regardless of particular content, would be formally classified "top secret-sensitive." Although many items in the study had previously been classified in various degrees by various officials, at this stage the rationale was simply that the very existence of the study was a secret; any page, no matter how innocuous, might betray its existence to an unauthorized person. No explicit reference was made to Executive Order No. 10501, which provided that information could be classified "top secret" only if disclosure "could result in exceptionally grave damage to the national security."

The designation "sensitive" was added informally to indicate that disclosure could produce bureaucratic and political embarrassment, apart from any effect the information might have on national security. (The word "sensitive" has no legal standing, since it nowhere appears in the executive order on classification or in the classification regulations of the Defense Department.)

The study in its final form began with a series of volumes summarizing American activities in Vietnam prior to the election of President Kennedy. The remaining volumes focused more intently on particular episodes and programs, including the Diem coup; the Gulf of Tonkin episode; the South Vietnamese request for American troops; the decision to deploy US forces in Vietnam and buildup of those forces; the decision to begin and expand bombing operations against North Vietnam; and the history of American negotiations with the North Vietnamese government, leading up to the opening of the Paris Peace talks in 1968.[2]

The early volumes are most interesting for what they reveal about official perceptions of Ho Chi Minh and the movement under his control. In the closing days of World War II, Ho sought American support for his war of independence, which he described as inspired by the American Revolution. Intelligence documents confirmed the strong nationalistic fervor of the movement in Indochina, and Ho's determination, despite his communist affiliation, to maintain independence from Soviet domination. American memoranda made clear that Washington officials recognized the strength of Ho's claim to legitimacy as the ruler of Vietnam. Nevertheless, the United States decided to support the French in reconquering Indochina. None of the above information was made public, because it would have jeopardized congressional support for large-scale military assistance to the French. Moreover, it would have clouded the picture of a monolithic communist menace, which supplied an essential premise of American foreign policy. The American public and the Congress were instead presented with a simplistic account, in which Ho figured as merely an agent of the Soviet Comintern.

The Pentagon Papers account of the 1963 coup against President Ngo Dinh Diem reveals that the Central Intelligence Agency was aware of the preparations for the coup and gave the plotters at least indirect encouragement and support. Certainly no effort was made to warn Diem, who, along with his brother, lost his life in the coup. While President Kennedy's public denial of American complicity may have been literally true, it did not represent a forthright disclosure of the actual American role. Secrecy served, in part, to avoid recriminations from American supporters of Diem, as well as those opposed in principle to violent interventions of this type. Of course, certain foreign governments would also have been exceedingly disturbed by proof of American duplicity toward a supposed ally.

During the 1964 presidential campaign, President Lyndon Johnson vigorously denounced the proposals of his Republican opponent, Barry Goldwater, to send American troops and planes into Vietnam. At the same time he would occasionally express , with much softer emphasis, his intent to see the struggle through to a successful conclusion. Johnson did not admit any inconsistency between his two positions. Yet the Pentagon Papers reveal that most of the President's advisers and particularly the Joint Chiefs of Staff had already concluded that an extensive American military involvement would be necessary to prevent a Vietcong victory in South Vietnam. The development of contingency plans for massive intervention went forward in secrecy during the campaign. Possibly the President had not yet finally made up his mind to implement these plans, although explicit threats to bomb North Vietnam were conveyed to Hanoi, via Canadian intermediaries, even before the election. It is certain, at any rate, that Lyndon Johnson misled the electorate by appearing to support a policy of victory without escalation, a policy that he did not in fact regard as a viable option.

Revealing his actual thinking prior to the election would have deprived Johnson of his most effective campaign issue, since there was little difference between Johnson's real views and those put forward by Goldwater. Of course, the deception had to be concealed after the election as well. To account for Johnson's postelection shift to a policy of intervention some apparent change in the situation in Vietnam was called for. The Gulf of Tonkin incident neatly fit the bill.

Confronted with this "unprovoked" attack on American ships, Congress rapidly approved a resolution authorizing American combat operations in Indochina and commencement of American bombing and infantry activities in Vietnam. But the Pentagon Papers reveal that a draft resolution had been prepared months in advance by the administration, and that United States and South Vietnamese vessels were engaging in extensive intelligence operations off the coast of North Vietnam up until the very night of the Tonkin Gulf episode. Both the unprovoked nature of the North Vietnamese action and the spontaneity of the administration's response were fabrication.

At the same time the attitude of the Saigon administration toward introduction of American troops in Vietnam was grossly misrepresented. The official U.S. position stated that the South Vietnamese had urgently requested the introduction of American forces, in response to externally supported and inspired aggression. In fact, the Pentagon Papers prove, the government of South Vietnam was extremely reluctant to permit the introduction of American forces, acquiescing only under extreme pressure from American Ambassador Maxwell Taylor. Like the Tonkin Gulf Resolution, the Vietnamese "request" was essentially prepared to order by the United States government. Clearly, proposals that the United States send in troops over the objections of the Saigon government would have provoked a major debate within the United States. The administration avoided that controversy by keeping the facts secret.

Finally, the military measures outlined above accompanied the Johnson administration's insistence that it was anxious to pursue a negotiated settlement of the conflict. The four "negotiating" volumes of the Pentagon Papers reveal that from 1964 to 1966 the administration felt it could negotiate only from a position of weakness, and this it was unwilling to do. Thus the secret messages conveyed to Hanoi, for example by Canadian officials, did not hold out the prospect of a compromise settlement. Rather, they warned Hanoi that it had to stop supporting the insurgents or suffer escalation of the war. These messages too were kept secret in order to uphold the pretense of the administration's sincere desire for negotiations.

Thus, the Pentagon Papers reveal a consistent pattern of deception by the administration, centered on withholding from Congress and the public vital information that raised devastating questions about the effectiveness and propriety of administration policies and the credibility of responsible officials. It is not hard to understand why, given the policies and rationales to which the government was committed, the Pentagon Papers had to be kept secret.

We should take note at this point of some things the Papers did not contain: There was nothing in the nature of weapons or electronics design information, identities of secret agents still in the field, or other material of the sort that could be of great value to foreign governments while of little relevance to public concerns. The secrecy of the study could not be justified on such straightforward grounds.[3]

Secretary of Defense Robert McNamara left office in March 1968. As a courtesy to McNamara, his successor, Clark Clifford, directed that the study be continued under the supervision of Assistant Secretary of Defense Paul Warnke. Later it became clear that the typing and reproduction of the study could not be completed before Johnson left office. As a precaution, Gelb, Warnke, and Halperin arranged for the twenty-eight volumes that had already been completed to be shipped to the Rand Corporation. However, Nixon's Secretary of Defense, Melvin Laird, made no effort to interfere with the typing, reproduction, or distribution of the study. The project was eventually finished under the supervision of the military assistants to the Defense Secretary who had continued in office despite the change of administration

It appears that at this time Laird and Hen.y Kissinger were the only senior officials of the Nixon administration who knew of the Pentagon Papers' existence. Kissinger had been told of it by Leslie Gelb at the inception of the study, while Kissinger was still a professor at Harvard. It was Gelb who, after consultation with others, now drew up the list of persons who would receive copies of the project. This list, which was approved by the Secretary's office, included eight former high officials of the Johnson administration, all of them now private citizens: Robert S. McNamara, Clark N. Clifford, Paul H. Nitze, Paul C. Warnke, Nicholas de B. Katzenbach, William P. Bundy, Leslie H. Gelb, and Morton H. Halperin;[4] a single copy went to Gelb and Halperin jointly. The distributed copies were to be stored in government-approved classified storage areas; others were simply locked up in the Defense Department and shown to no one.

The copies supplied to Warnke and to Gelb and Halperin were deposited in a government-approved classified storage facility at the Rand Corporation, along with the partial set sent there during the Johnson administration. Under a special arrangement negotiated between the three former officials and Rand President Henry Rowan, Rand could use the studies for its research only with the specific permission of any two of those officials. Daniel Ellsberg, who had worked on the Pentagon Papers and was now writing a Rand study of the history of American involvement in Indochina, asked for access to the volumes. After some discussion, Halperin and Gelb gave the necessary permission. Ellsberg took the volumes from the Rand Washington Office out to Rand Headquarters in Santa Monica and read them there.

Ellsberg was profoundly shocked by the evidence of deception and incptitude collected in the papers. He concluded that the facts ought to be brought before the American people, and with Anthony Russo, an antiwar Rand employee, he copied one or two volumes each day at a local advertising agency. In so doing, the "top secret-sensitive" designation was covered at Ellsberg's direction and not reproduced. In spring of 1970 a complete set was delivered to Senator William Fulbright, chairman of the Senate Foreign Relations Committee, in the hope that public hearings would follow. The senator felt unable to make public use of the information, however, because he did not wish to appear to condone the unorthodox procedure whereby the study had reached him. Instead, Fulbright wrote to Secretary of Defense Melvin Laird requesting a copy, but giving no hint of how he knew of its existence.

Laird wrote Fulbright that it would not be in the interest of national security to make the study available to the Foreign Relations Committee, even on a classified basis. The Secretary did not formally claim "executive privilege," nor did he invoke any specific legal or factual basis for his decision. We can only speculate as to his motives: Insofar as the policies of the Nixon administration were continuous with those debunked in the papers, the prospect of disclosure must still have seemed very unappealing. Fulbright protested Laird's decision in vain and then decided to let the matter drop. Perhaps he believed that peace was imminent, and there would be little to gain by besmirching the record of former Democratic administrations. Or perhaps he simply lacked the political leverage to win an overt battle to force release of the study.

At this point, however, *New York Times* reporter Neil Sheehan came into possession of a set of the Pentagon Papers, complete except for the four "negotiating" volumes. For the *Times* as much as for Senator Fulbright, the acquisition was an extraordinary and potentially embarrassing event. But after much debate, the editors and publishers of the *New York Times* decided to go forward with publication. They proceeded with a degree of secrecy that the study's authors might have envied. Only a very small number of *Times* personnel knew of the project. The newspaper rented a hotel room in Manhattan, where Sheehan and a few others read through the volumes and produced a series of stories that first appeared in print on Sunday, June 13, 1971, under a modest headline.

Sunday brought no reaction, but on Monday Attorney General John Mitchell sent a telegram to the *New York Times'* publishers, asking them to cease publication of the series and to return the documents in their possession to the Defense Department. When the *Times* refused, the government took the unprecedented step of going into federal court in New York and asking for an injunction against publication. The government relied in large part on secret written briefs, which were provided to the lawyers for the *Times,* but which have not been made public to this day. While the case was before the court, the *Times* was temporarily enjoined from continuing the publication of its series. Meanwhile, the *Washington Post,* which had also obtained copies of some of the volumes, began publication as well, provoking a second injunction suit by the executive branch. Seventeen days after the New York injunction went into effect, the Supreme Court lifted both injunctions and held that the First Amendment guaranteed the newspapers' right to publish the material in question. However, a clear majority of the Court expressed the view that prior restraint is permissible in certain extreme circumstances.[5]

The position taken by the courts in the civil litigation, augmented by public and congressional clamor, impelled the executive branch to publish official versions of the remaining volumes—except for the "negotiating" volumes—after a formal declassification review by the Pentagon Office of Security Review. However, the official version omitted certain material that appeared in an unofficial version published by Beacon Press (the "Gravel Edition") as well as in the *New York Times.*[6] Moreover, the *Washington Post* apparently acceded to government requests not to publish certain specific material.

On the eve of the Supreme Court hearing on the injunctions, the government opened a second legal front by filing a criminal complaint against Daniel Ellsberg for theft and espionage in connection with the release of the Pentagon papers. Subsequently, Ellsberg and Anthony Russo both were reindicted on eighteen counts of espionage, conspiracy, and theft. That case was dismissed after five months of trial because of government misconduct, when it became known that the investigation of Ellsberg had included such unorthodox measures as an attempt to smear him and his lawyers, a burglary of his psychiatrist's office, preparation of a psychological profile of Ellsberg by the CIA, and concealment of the fact that Ellsberg had been overheard on an irregular electronic surveillance. Thus, with no definitive interpretation, the scope of the espionage law remains in doubt, leaving open the threat of future indictments against loyal citizens who leak or publish classified information.[7]

The drastic steps taken against Ellsberg were not an isolated case. The wiretap on which Ellsberg was overheard proved to have been one of seventeen taps placed on the phones of newspapermen and government officials to investigate an unspecified leak. Only later was this leak identified as a news story, given no credence at the time, disclosing that the United States was secretly bombing Cambodia on a massive scale.

The Secret Bombing of Cambodia

On Sunday, March 16, 1969, President Richard Nixon and about six senior national security advisers approved a proposal to bomb neutral Cambodia. Their decision, and the fifteen-month bombing operation that followed, remained secret for more than three years from most officials of the executive branch, from all but a few members of Congress, and from the public.[8]

The proposal to bomb Cambodia was not a new one. Ever since President Lyndon Johnson had escalated the American intervention in Vietnam in 1965, the Joint Chiefs of Staff had repeatedly recommended such an action, as well as ground operations in Laos, Cambodia, and North Vietnam and the mining of Haiphong Harbor. To the extent that these proposals were known, there was substantial congressional and public support for them. In well publicized hearings before the Senate Armed Services Committee, the Joint Chiefs' requests to bomb additional targets in North Vietnam were sympathetically received, and subsequently this authority was largely granted by President Johnson.[9]

Although the formal proposals to bomb Cambodia were all stamped "Top Secret," it was widely known in Washington that the Joint Chiefs favored this further expansion of the war. They eagerly testified in secret before congressional committees, using the argument that from the military perspective, targets in Cambodia were part of the theater of operations. The North Vietnamese and Viet-Cong forces were using Cambodian territory as a sanctuary for base camps and supply lines.

Civilian officials of the Johnson administration, however, doubted that even a sustained bombing campaign would do much good. Intensive bombing in South Vietnam, North Vietnam, and Laos had not succeeded in preventing the movement of supplies or in effectively curtailing enemy attacks. Moreover, the independent and neutral status of Cambodia introduced serious diplomatic and legal obstacles to an acknowledged military operation in that country. For those reasons the skeptics sought to avoid public discussion of proposals to widen the war, fearing that pressure from hawkish elements in the public and Congress would secure implementation of those plans.

By the closing months of the Johnson administration, public opinion had shifted in a dovish direction. The outgoing President responded by curtailing and then ending the bombing of North Vietnam. The Joint Chiefs, sensitive to the mood of the administration and the country, did not press for a reversal of these actions nor did they then renew proposals to bomb Cambodia.

It was the inauguration of Richard Nixon on January 20, 1969, that brought these proposals back to life. The military will routinely submit proposals previously rejected by civilian officials to a new President or Secretary of Defense. Thus, on February 11, 1969, General Creighton Abrams, commander of U.S. forces in Vietnam, recommended and requested authorization to conduct B-52 strikes in Cambodia. The Joint Chiefs forwarded this proposal to the President through Secretary of Defense Melvin Laird. The memorandum, once again, was stamped "Top Secret"; this time neither testimony to Congress nor conversations with the press hinted that the military were seeking to escalate the war. Although some potential congressional and public support for escalation still existed, the military had reason to believe that by now the great majority of the public opposed expansion of the war. The new President's attitude, however, remained to be discovered; the indicated tactic was one of quiet persuasion.

Richard Nixon needed no convincing. The incoming President and his principal foreign policy adviser, Henry Kissinger, were already bent upon a Vietnam strategy favorable to the Joint Chiefs. It called for two very different messages, one to Hanoi and its allies and the other to the American people. The public would be led to believe that the United States was withdrawing from Vietnam. At the same time the North Vietnamese must be convinced that the United States would escalate the war unless it was settled on terms satisfactory to Washington.

Secrecy was an essential ingredient of this strategy. Certain members of the executive branch, if they learned of threats or contingency plans to escalate the conflict, might bring these to the attention of Congress and the public. Undoubtedly, a great public outcry would signal Hanoi that Nixon could not carry through his threats. Congress might even pass legislation making escalation illegal and mandating a speedy withdrawal of American forces.

Thus the Nixon-Kissinger plan was disclosed to the smallest conceivable circle of advisers. Initially, this consisted of a small group on the National Security Council staff and in the Pentagon and CIA. After the decision to bomb Cambodia was made, the circle had to be expanded somewhat. The Secretaries of State and Defense were brought into the picture along with their personal staffs; certain military officers in the field also had to do the detailed planning for the attacks.

There was some military advantage to be gained from initial surprise, but the Pentagon had not proposed or expected that an ongoing bombing program would be kept secret. That decision came from, and served the political requirements of, the President and his White House national security adviser. Their directive, ordering the commencement of B-52 bombing raids under the code name of MENU OPERATIONS, provided for the strictest secrecy. Knowledge of the operation was limited to those who had a "need-to-know" in order to carry out the bombing campaign, while others, including officials within the executive branch, were excluded. To account for the bombing sorties actually flown, the missions in Cambodia were reported, through classified channels, as if they had occurred in South Vietnam. Accurate reports were transmitted through a separate, limited "black channel." Even officials with "Top Secret" clearances, including the Secretary of the Air Force, were deceived. General Earle Wheeler, Chairman of the Joint Chiefs, later told the Senate Armed Services Committee that, had the Secretary asked him about it directly, Wheeler would have regarded it as his duty to lie about the bombing.

Of course, those who deceived their colleagues had few qualms about misleading Congress and the public. Prior to May 1, 1970 (when the United States publicly initiated ground and air operations in Cambodia), Congress and the public had been frequently assured that that country's neutrality was being strictly respected. This was the position taken in secret congressional testimony, as well as in public speeches of the President and others. For example, in his nationally televised speech on April 30, 1970, announcing the American invasion, President Nixon told the American people with regard to enemy bases in Cambodia that:

> For 5 years, neither the United States nor South Vietnam has moved against these enemy sanctuaries because we did not wish to violate the territory of a neutral nation. Even after the Vietnamese communists began to expand these sanctuaries 4 weeks ago, we counselled patience to our South Vietnamese allies and imposed restraints on our own commanders.[10]

Between March 18, 1969, and May 1, 1970, 3,695 B-52 sorties had in fact dropped some 105,837 tons of bombs on Cambodia. This was not disclosed even after May 1. The MENU OPERATIONS were not officially acknowledged by the administration until July 16, 1973, and even then the disclosure was not voluntary and spontaneous, but a grudging admission of what had become known despite vigorous attempts at concealment.

The White House did claim in 1973 that thirteen "key" members of the Senate and House—all vigorous proponents of escalation— had been apprised of the bombing as early as March 1969. It is curious that of the nine members from this list still living in 1973, only four could definitely recall having been informed, while three others firmly denied it. At any rate it is certain that the established procedures for providing secret information to responsible congressional committees were not involved; no debate was held in which opposing views could have been presented. And whatever informal "consultations" occurred did not entail a meaningful accountability to the electorate for this program, either on the part of the members allegedly involved or of Congress as a whole.

The systematic, illicit efforts to keep the MENU OPERATIONS secret were not entirely successful, but they committed the White House so fully to a course of secrecy that measures even more drastic were necessary to prevent calamitous embarrassment. On May 9, 1969, a front-page article in the *New York Times,* by Pentagon correspondent William Beecher, reported that the United States had begun bombing Cambodia. Pentagon spokesmen refused to confirm the *Times* report, and neither Congress nor the press cared to pursue the matter further. In the re'atively trusting pre-Watergate atmosphere, the story was simply unbelievable. The administration's strategy—persuading the public that it was ending the war—had succeeded so well that, without official confirmation of the *Times* story, no one was prepared to pursue its allegations.

However, the Beecher article prompted suspicion that there might be a serious leak in the innermost councils of government. National Security Adviser Kissinger telephoned FBI Director J. Edgar Hoover to request an investigation. Without seeking judicial warrants, a series of wiretaps was initiated, eventually covering the phones of seventeen government officials and reporters; the program lasted for twenty-one months. No evidence of leaks was ever uncovered, nor has the source of the Beecher story ever been identified.[11]

In May 1973 the story of the wiretaps surfaced dramatically in the press, when the interception of Ellsberg on one of the taps was reported at the Pentagon Papers criminal trial. Still the administration would not admit to the Cambodian bombing operations; some other explanation for the taps was necessary. Although other leaks were cited, these did not convincingly explain the surveillance program either in terms of their timing or magnitude.

By this time the political forces working for disclosure had reached irresistible proportions. The decisive step finally was taken by one Major Knight, who repented of his role in forging after-action reports to hide the Cambodian bombing. Knight's letter to a senator led to the successful questioning of the Air Force Chief of Staff, General George Brown; and the candid testimony of that officer was confirmed in writing by Defense Secretary James Schlesinger.

High officials of the State and Defense departments hastened to deny responsibility for the deception, stating that they had not recommended secrecy. The White House, unable to join in the general round of buck-passing, finally claimed it had been protecting the then Cambodian leader, Prince Sihanouk. The Prince had acquiesced in the bombings, White House spokesmen implied, on condition that they be kept secret. If the United States had announced its missions, Henry Kissinger explained to the Senate Foreign Relations committee, Prince Sihanouk would have been forced to protest; the United States would have had to halt the bombing.

This rationale on diplomatic grounds was subject to numerous serious objections:

The Nixon administration never produced solid evidence that it had negotiated with Sihanouk about the bombing. Hints that an agreement took shape in conversations between Sihanouk and Chester Bowles or Mike Mansfield brought prompt denials from the Americans named.

The Cambodian government in 1969 and 1970 had in fact frequently protested to the UN about the acknowledged American policy of allowing our fighter planes to cross their border while engaged in "hot pursuit." These complaints received almost no press attention in the United States and were successsfully ignored by the Nixon administration, suggesting that protests about B-52 bombings could also have been ignored.

The assertion that public outcry, even if embarrassing, would have forced the United States to stop the bombing was simply disingenuous. For one thing, there remained the justification that the area under attack was entirely under North Vietnamese control and that no Cambodians lived in the area. The administration could have offered to stop the bombing as soon as Sihanouk regained control of the territory and prevented Hanoi from using it as a base camp. Beyond this, it is unclear why our hands would have been tied by world public opinion over Cambodia when they were not in the case of North Vietnam.

The explanation offered by the White House did not even pretend to justify the continued secrecy and deception after May 1970. By then, Sihanouk had been deposed. The United States was publicly bombing Cambodia at the request of the new government, which had condemned Sihanouk for collaborating with the North Vietnamese. A public admission of the earlier bombing would not have embarrassed the new leaders.

The administration's rationale did not explain the need to deceive high U.S. officials and congressional committees who were taking testimony in secret session or the need to engage in illegal wiretapping.

In fact, the President's argument seemed to suggest that an emergency whose very existence is secret justifies illegal measures that are also secret, and that none of this need ever be revealed. In confining himself to the assertion that it was not possible to bomb openly, the President failed entirely to meet the contention that, therefore, he should not have bombed at all. Indeed, the White House rationale went well beyond the difficult, if ancient proposition that in emergencies, it is proper for a President to set aside constitutional limitations if he "throws himself upon the country" for approval at the earliest opportunity. For no voluntary disclosure was made or ratification sought until long after any conceivable emergency had passed.

All in all, it was difficult to escape the conclusion that the real reason for four years of deception was simply to prevent Congress and the public from performing their constitutional roles in declaring war, appropriating funds, raising and supporting armies, debating policy guidelines, and evaluating the performance of elected officials. The President's total disregard for the constitutional values at stake prompted the House Judiciary Committee to consider an impeachment article based upon the secret bombing. That article was not accepted by the committee, because of the feeling that prior administrations, and Congress as well, were in large measure responsible for creating a climate in which such conduct may have appeared permissible.[12] Nevertheless, most members agreed that the President's conduct was indeed highly improper.

Following Richard Nixon's resignation the political climate changed dramatically. Secrecy appeared to carry such risks, both for Presidents and for the bureaucracy, that some observers thought that the problems of excessive secrecy had greatly shrunk, if not vanished altogether.

The abuses of the past were attributed in part to the personalities of Richard Nixon and Lyndon Johnson. Both were said to be unusually secretive men, whose private inclinations were reinforced by the knowledge that they were pursuing policies that lacked public support. Gerald Ford, in contrast, was considered to be "the most open President since George Washington"; his administration, it was promised, would not be marred by attempts to keep important initiatives hidden.

Moreover, it was said, secrecy in the past had been encouraged by public indifference. In the post Vietnam/Watergate era, the executive branch would not dare to try to keep secrets and in any case would not succeed. On the contrary, executive officials argued vigorously that the pendulum had swung too far toward openness. They not only resisted efforts to liberalize the formal secrecy system, but insisted on the need to tighten it in the name of national security. The Nixon administration had asserted as much after the Pentagon Papers episode, and the Ford administration continued the argument as well.

Intervention in Angola

Any illusions that the problem of secrecy had been solved were shattered by the disclosure that the Ford administration had secretly intervened in a civil war in Angola. Although the episode became public much more quickly than it might have in the past, this was not because the President or the bureaucrats volunteered the information. Nor did disclosure occur soon enough to avert a serious embarrassment for American foreign policy.[13]

In the spring of 1975, with the Portuguese determined to withdraw from Angola and grant the African nation its independence, violence erupted among three groups competing for power. One group, the MPLA, had been receiving substantial Soviet aid for years in its struggle against Portugal. The other two groups were being helped by pro-Western African governments.

At this point a debate took place within the administration—confined effectively within the President's inner circle and the bureaucratic subsystem relating to covert operations—about whether to aid the factions opposing the MPLA. Few if any in Congress or the public had any idea what was being discussed before a decision was reached.

Indeed, when Assistant Secretary of State for African Affairs Nathaniel Davis resigned, no one even suspected that his resignation was connected with Angola. Neither the formal secrecy system, the informal code of officialdom, nor the "new" political climate impelled this official to make public his reasons for leaving the administration.

The decision to give military assistance to two factions in the Angolan civil war, potentially creating a serious great-power confrontation, was made without any public debate about the importance of Angola to the United States or the implications of a victory there by one faction or another. Nor was there discussion of the impact of this operation on the prospects for continued détente, for normalization of relations with Cuba (now heavily involved in assisting the MPLA), and for improved relations with other African and Latin American countries. It is true that, as required by legislation passed in 1974, six congressional committees were later notified that a small covert operation was already under way. (These committees—the armed services, appropriations, and foreign relations committees of each house—have established small subcommittees to receive CIA briefings about covert operations.) In this instance, many of those briefed were incredulous that the United States had in 1975 taken on such a commitment in secret. Those who opposed the action, however, felt unable to make the operation public. Short of so doing, they saw no way to stop the intervention.

During the fall of 1975 Senator Dick Clark, Chairman of the subcommittee on Africa of the Senate Foreign Relations Committee, learned about the covert program under way in Angola. He asked for and received a full briefing on the program, but he too felt that he could not discuss the program in public or seek to stop it at this point.

Only after subsequent reports of the American operation appeared in the press to the accompaniment of a great public outcry, was prohibitory legislation introduced by Senators Clark and John Tunney. The Senate, after a secret session and over the strong objections of the President and the Secretary of State, voted to end all American assistance to Angola. In January 1976 the House sustained the Senate action. Much of the opposition in Congress was based on the specifics of the Angolan situation, but it was bolstered and embittered by the secrecy of the attempted intervention.

The administration's attempt to confront Congress with a *fait accompli* ended in great embarrassment, which could have been avoided by timely consultations. The "lessons of Vietnam," it would seem, are not easily learned by energetic officials, no matter how conscientious. When pressed to explain its actions, the administration's reply was no more convincing than had been Richard Nixon's defense of the secret bombing of Cambodia. Spokesmen claimed that the American objective in Angola was simply to bring about a negotiated withdrawal of Soviet and Cuban troops and the formation of a representative, indigenous government. To do so meant a) maintaining a military balance of power and b) avoiding an open confrontation, from which the Soviets would not back down. Thus, there had to be military intervention, and it had to be secret.

This simplistic argument ignored the meaning that American secrecy would have for Soviet decision-makers. Covert American intervention would lead the Soviets to conclude that the operation lacked substantial backing in the United States. A public commitment might have been taken more seriously by the Soviets. As it was, they proceeded to escalate the scale of the conflict to the point where the American military assistance could not be kept secret, and in fact it was the Ford administration that was forced to back down. It is difficult to escape the conclusion that the Angolan intervention was kept secret not to help the Russians get out, but to help the Americans get in.

Drawing Conclusions

In the aftermath of these episodes, many outside the executive bureaucracy have come to agree on the need to reexamine the way our government balances the public's right to know against the requirements of secrecy. The lessons of these three cases seem very clear. The executive branch today has the capacity to conceal, for substantial periods of time, information that would significantly contribute to legitimate public debate on major issues. Recent Presidents, however diverse in personal character and political circumstance, have all betrayed a disposition to use this power of secrecy in ways that are hard to justify in terms of straightforward national security concerns. The results have been costly for the nation at home and abroad, as secrecy has delayed the correction of divisive and irrational policies. In some cases, moreover, the attempt to prevent or punish unwelcome disclosures has led to significant infringements of our civil liberties.

These cases are not merely aberrations. Rather, they represent the most dramatic aspects of a systemic and continuing problem, as we shall see in Chapter 3.

Chapter 3

Inside the Secrecy System

Governmental secrecy is as old as government itself but the details of the contemporary secrecy system in America reflect the particular forces that have shaped our recent history.[1]

Secrecy in national security affairs has seldom been a central issue in American political life. Historically, there was little to keep secret from other governments and little clamor at home for greater access to decision-making. When crises did arise, the country was apt to rally in support of administration policy. In wartime, voluntary censorship was accepted with little fuss, and the return of peace always witnessed a rapid relaxation of these restraints.

Because secrecy was not institutionalized, it became an issue only rarely, when current administration policy encountered heated opposition, usually on a partisan basis. Where private citizens' demands for information could be simply ignored, such demands by Congress had powerful constitutional sanction and had to be answered. (See Chapter 6 below.) Thus, the historic debates about secrecy typically involved conflicts between the branches of government, instigated by party leaders who tended to manipulate the issue in the service of immediate policy goals. The development of a rational, principled approach to the secrecy problem was not the primary concern of the protagonists, and the passing of the immediate crises tended to cut short the discussion of secrecy as well.

Long before the twentieth century, a pattern of flexible pragmatism concerning secrecy and publicity became well established. To a large extent, the vicissitudes of the political party system shaped the course of events. A Congress controlled by the President's party was likely to grant him a relatively broad zone of discretion, while an opposition-controlled Congress would feel less inhibited in insisting on its prerogatives. Thus, the claims asserted by the parties varied widely as did the immediate outcomes of various episodes. The underlying flexible pattern, however, remained stable for many years.

It was not until the Cold War era that the nation moved decisively away from the traditional system of informal controls. Prompted by deep concern for foreign and domestic security, policy makers felt an uncommonly intense need for secrecy, a concern that seemed to call for measures unprecedented in peace time.

This imperative was augmented by profound and permanent changes in the structure of the executive branch. Where in the early days, those with access, or even seeking access, to national security information numbered only a few easily identified and politically accountable officials, today a vast bureaucracy makes and implements policy. This growth introduced to security and publicity problems a quantitative dimension that the traditional system of informal, face-to-face controls could not absorb. Both the need to keep sensitive information out of enemy hands and the need for unity in policy-making seemed to call for a carefully structured system of information control.

In 1951, President Truman issued a sweeping executive order, designed to institutionalize the system of military secrecy that had developed during World War II, and to extend it, under presidential control, to the civilian agencies of government. His program was vigorously criticized in many of its details, but the basic propriety of the action was not seriously challenged. On the whole, Congress, the press, and most of the attentive public accepted the need for substantial secrecy and for strong presidential leadership in the struggle against international communism. The tradition of wartime military censorship, extending back to the War of 1812, seemed to support the unilateral action of the President, and many of the specific objections to the system were defused by a revised order issued by President Eisenhower in 1953.

Fundamentally the system established in the early 1950s is that prevailing today. The process of keeping secrets and releasing information operates at two different levels. Though the two levels overlap somewhat in practice, it is easier to consider them separately. The first centers around the President and involves a small amount of critical information on major policy issues. The second level is in the bureaucracy, which routinely handles vast quantities of information according to the procedures of the Executive Order on Classification.

While the abuses of the bureaucratic system in overclassifying information are well attested, it is presidential secrecy that has the most dangerous and direct effect on public debate on foreign policy issues. Successful reform clearly must reach both levels.

The Presidential Secrecy System

In his discussions with President-elect Richard Nixon, outgoing President Lyndon Johnson warned that the success of his policies would depend on preventing leaks of information from the bureaucracy.[2] This advice was not unusual. All of our postwar Presidents, bolstered by the belief that they had the right to decide what information about national security matters to give to Congress and the public, have been concerned about leaks. Moreover, they have treated this as a matter of discretion, outside the formal rules of the bureaucratic classification system. The President and his top associates have believed that they are free to determine on an *ad-hoc* basis whether or not to keep information secret. Senior officials are usually not familiar with the criteria and procedures for classification contained in the Executive Order on Classification and on the whole do not follow them.[3] Their documents are usually stamped "Secret" or "Top Secret," but even this formality sometimes is not followed.

If Presidents do not feel bound by the procedures of the executive order in deciding what to keep secret, neither do they rely on them to safeguard the information they want kept out of public view. A primary technique used to maintain presidential secrecy is simply to narrow drastically the circle of those consulted. An extreme example was the planning by the Nixon administration for a change in China policy. For a long time the new strategy was known only to the President; his national security advisor, Henry Kissinger; his chief staff assistant, H. R. Haldeman; and one member of Kissinger's staff. The bombing of Cambodia was planned by a group almost as small, and this practice was by no means limited to the Nixon administration. President Johnson had made many decisions relating to Vietnam at the Tuesday lunch, a small informal group of his top advisers. Approval of covert operations has often been the work of very small groups. The same is true of the conduct of certain important negotiations, such as the Salt agreements, not to mention the management of great international crises in Berlin, Cuba, and the Middle East.

When these kinds of plans are ready for implementation a wider circle, including many people in the permanent bureaucracy, must be informed and yet somehow persuaded to keep the information secret. In many cases Presidents have not been prepared to rely on the formal bureaucratic secrecy system. What they try to do was spelled out most vividly by Richard Nixon in a small meeting in his office shortly after the *New York Times* began publishing the Pentagon Papers. The White House taping system recorded the President's views:

> *President*: And maybe another approach to it would be to set up and remember I already mentioned to set up a new classification. . . . Which we would call what? Let's just call it a new classifica—Don't use TOP SECRET for me ever again. I never want to see TOP SECRET in this God damn office. I think we just solved— shall we call it—Uh, John, what would be a good name?
> "President's Secure—" Or, uh—"Eyes Only" is a silly thing too. It doesn't mean anything anymore. Uh—
> *Krogh:* We used "Presidential Document," before with one of the counsel we were working with, but that didn't—There's some
> *Ehrlichman:* How about—Uh, uh, looking forward to the court

case, I wonder if we could get the words "National Security" in
it.
President: Yeah.
Ehrlichman: So that "National," uh, just say "National Security
Classified" or "National Security— . . .
President: Well, uh, not the word "Secret" should not be used.
. . . Because you see "Secret" has been now compromised. What
I am getting at is this: I want a new classification for that
purpose and everything that I consider important, and only
those things I consider important will have that classification.
Then on that classification every document that is out is to be
numbered. You see what I mean? There's the—and the people—
so that we'll know what people have it. . . . Nobody is to have
access to the "President Cla—" or, uh, uh, no— "National
Security." Uh, "National Security"—no. And that's—Why
don't we just say "National Security"? I—Maybe you're right.
"National Se—Security"—not TOP SECRET. "National
Security," uh—or "Special National Security," or, uh, it's
something like that. But anyway, get that. So that it's just three
letters. Like, uh, "SN s—," "SNS" or something like that. . . .
Or, uh—And then on those, that kind of a thing. As I say, let's
limit the number of people that get it. We know who'll get it,
and then everybody who gets must sign the, the agreement to
take a polygraph.[4]

When the President needs to share information with the
bureaucracy but still has a strong interest in keeping it secret, he may
impose special restrictions on access to the information, beyond the
normal requirements of the bureaucratic secrecy system. In some
cases, specialized subsystems of the bureaucratic secrecy system are
available. Thus, there are systems connected with intelligence
gathering that require special clearance and access procedures. These
were used to safeguard information relating to covert actions in Chile
and Angola.

Where such special access systems do not exist, they can be
created on an *ad hoc* basis. Generally the President or his closest
advisers will draw up a list of names of those who are to have access to
a special presidential secret. A code word is selected for the operation;
and all cables and memoranda related to the operation are "slugged"

with that code word. Thus Vietnam negotiating cables in the Johnson administration went under the heading "Harvan," and Cambodian bombing cables were slugged "MENU OPERATION." Such messages move in separate channels and are seen only by those with authorized access—persons whose disposition to cooperate with the presidential policy has been carefully evaluated.

If the information does somehow escape the confines of the executive branch, the administrative techniques outlined above are no longer relevant. Of course, the President can still attempt to persuade members of Congress or the press not to disclose the information. But at this stage his control of the situation is much more tenuous, because the authority of his office cannot be conclusively invoked.

Until recently Presidents had sought to enforce secrecy only by means of their own authority within the executive branch, plus whatever informal pressures could be brought to bear on outsiders to accept a degree of self-censorship. As noted above, access to information was often severely limited. When leaks occurred, efforts were made to track them down and to exclude from future access those who had not respected the Presidents' definition of what should be secret. In some instances wiretaps and other forms of surveillance as well as lie detectors were used to find the breakdown in security.[5]

Beginning with the Pentagon Papers episode in 1971, Presidents have sought the assistance of the courts in enforcing secrecy. In our discussion of the Pentagon Papers, we mentioned the efforts first to enjoin publication of the papers and then the criminal prosecution of Daniel Ellsberg for his role in their release. The ambiguous results have led to subsequent presidential efforts to bolster this aspect of the secrecy system by requests for new legislation.[6]

The President's control of information can be used not only to preserve secrecy indefinitely, but also to delay publication until the most propitious time, in terms of the President's interests. Thus President Nixon announced his new China policy by disclosing that his national security adviser Henry Kissinger had just come back from Peking and that he himself would soon visit China.

Sometimes presidential discretion may dictate the release of information that is treated as very highly classsified in the bureaucratic system. At the time of the Cuban missile crisis, for example, President Kennedy ordered the release of U-2 photographs taken over Cuba to demonstrate that there were Soviet missiles in Cuba. These photographs would never have been released without the President's intervention. There is nothing irregular about a judgment of this kind, if it is founded on foreign policy concerns. Yet presidential release of "classified" information sometimes has more ambiguous motives, and often it is done clandestinely in the form of leaks. James Reston has observed that the American ship of state is the only sailing vessel that leaks from the top. Presidential leaks to reporters, directly or through trusted aides, are commonplace on the Washington scene.

We shall return to a more extensive discussion of leaks after we have described the bureaucratic system. Here we note only that none of our postwar Presidents has exhibited a commitment to make information public whenever this would facilitate debate on key issues. Release of information, in whatever manner, has been viewed as a presidential prerogative to be employed when it advances his interests. This is true to an even greater degree when it comes to withholding information.

The purpose of secrecy sometimes relates to considerations of national security, but often it derives from a domestic political need. The President may recognize that if secrecy is not maintained, a proposed policy or action will encounter vigorous opposition within the bureaucracy, from Congress, or from the public. Thus Presidents have often used secrecy to exclude those groups from decisions and actions of great consequence. Besides the cases discussed in Chapter Two, important actions concealed in recent years include the secret American war in Laos, American commitments to Spain, and American support for the Kurds in Iraq.

Less controversial, but surely no less fateful, has been the performance of postwar Presidents and/or top-level presidential envoys in the conduct of major negotiations and crisis-management. For better or for worse, these grave responsibilities have often been undertaken without a prior sampling of opinion even within the relevant bureaucracies, much less within Congress or the nation at large. In the most extreme case, an emissary holding no constitutional office may conduct delicate negotiations outside the nation's borders and under minimal supervision from Washington.

While we recognize that national security concerns give rise to a legitimate need for some secrecy, it would seem that the unchecked practice of presidential discretion—often unavoidably delegated to senior advisers—has led to abuses, mistakes, and setbacks for national unity and self-confidence, if not for national security as well. We are persuaded that these shortcomings are systemic, and not due entirely to the flaws of particular persons. No President and no official has built-in incentive to spend time and resources publicizing his or her actions, without carefully weighing the potential for arousing needless opposition, criticism, and distraction. On the contrary, occasions for publicity are carefully selected for their value in placing oneself in the best light—or perhaps one's opposition in the worst.

But any meaningful reform must address not only the Presidential abuses we have described but also those of the bureaucratic system.

The Bureaucratic Secrecy System

As the sociologist Max Weber long ago observed, secrecy is an occupational disease endemic to bureaucracy. Officials typically prefer to be left alone; they view secrecy as the best protection against outside interference in their activities.[7] This penchant for secrecy is reinforced, in the case of the foreign affairs staff, by the belief that the national security benefits by keeping as much information as possible from other governments.

The bureaucratic secrecy system is much more formally structured and routinized than is the presidential practice of secrecy. It currently rests on Executive Order No. 11652, promulgated by President Nixon on March 10, 1972, and on a series of implementing directives issued by the National Security Council and each concerned department. The directives create a complex system with three levels of classification—Top Secret, Secret, and Confidential—and elaborate procedures for classifying and declassifying documents.

In overview, the formal system is heavily biased toward secrecy. Any information may be kept classified if its release "could reasonably be expected to cause damage to the national security." The bureaucrat is not required to balance the expectation of harm against the public's right to know. Indeed, the executive order can be read, and often is read, as not even permitting such considerations. Thus an official who believes that disclosure of information could cause some damage, no matter how small, feels free, if not obliged, to classify a document.

There is no external check on this system. Officials know that they will not be reprimanded for overclassifying. There are no formal review procedures of significance. In practice, senior officials always prefer that junior officials err on the side of secrecy, not only because of the general preference for secrecy but also because a decision to classify, if it later appears mistaken, can easily be reversed. Information once released, however, cannot be called back.

Unlike the President, bureaucrats do feel bound by the rules of the classification system; but they see that system as providing wide room for what they call "judgment." The exercise of that judgment is powerfully shaped by the organizational environment, a leading characteristic of which is the-incessant bureaucratic struggle for power.

Observers often assume that the federal bureaucracy is a monolithic entity. In fact, it consists of innumerable organizations, cliques, and individuals engaged in constant battle for policy influence, larger budget shares, and other goods. A powerful weapon in that struggle is control over information. To put our contention very simply, important information is made public when someone in a position to release it decides that it would further his policy, organizational, or personal interests to do so. Much information is therefore kept secret not as a result of any evil intent, but simply because no one has a specific interest in its disclosure.

When bureaucratic interests can be enhanced by leaking

information to Congress or the public, officials have often done so, and they will continue to do so in the future. But informing the public on a systematic and principled basis is not a central purpose of any vested interest in the national security bureaucracy. In general, members of bureaucratic organizations tend to identify the interests of the public as a whole with those of their own group, as perceived by the dominant career personnel.[8] This means that outside consultation is not only potentially a nuisance, but that it is unnecessary: Senior officials themselves are the best judges of the public interest.

Although an official may cultivate an image of openness for the sake of his credibility and influence, few officials have so strong a commitment to that principle that they would jeopardize a favored policy, the prestige of their institution, or their own career for the sake of informing Congress or the public. On the contrary, the essence of the bureaucratic attitude is that secrecy is the rule, disclosure the exception.

This attitude has resulted in keeping secret a wide variety of information, some of it on important subjects such as the storage of nuclear weapons abroad, the organization and functions of various intelligence organizations, and plans to develop particular weapons systems.

The classification system does not in itself provide authority for withholding information from Congress; but congressional committees often do experience resistance in getting access to classified information. Clearly, this affects their ability to make a case against administration programs. Nor are these problems limited to situations in which the President is immediately responsible for the decision to withhold.

In fact, the bureaucratic secrecy system can be, and has been, used to keep information even from the President, at least temporarily. Thus, the preparation of the Pentagon Papers study was carefully kept secret from the White House; and it appears that significant covert operations have also been conducted without presidential knowledge.

Prompted by intrabureaucratic rivalries, officials generally seek to keep control over information as far as possible and to deny access to others—even supervisors—who might be tempted to oppose their programs or criticize their mistakes. The ability to narrow that circle is enhanced by the "need to know" provision of the executive order, which provides that even an official with an appropriate security clearance may not be given access to information he does not need to perform official duties. Thus, the Pentagon regularly denied information to the Arms Control and Disarmament Agency on weapons developments until congressional legislation established the agency's need to know.

Bureaucracies prefer, however, not to rely on the "need to know" provision. Instead they tend to develop their own, specialized classification systems, which they can completely control and which will provide tighter protection for their information. By creating special designators and special dissemination channels, the bureaucracy generating the information determines what classification levels should be used and who shall have access to the information. Someone who wants the information must apply for a clearance to the controlling bureaucracy and must promise not to disclose the information. Often enough, even the existence of the special system is unknown to those who lack the necessary clearances, which needless to say, creates something of a vicious cycle. It makes it difficult for even very high-ranking officials to discover that there are important things they do not know.

Two specialized systems, relating to cryptography and atomic energy, are authorized by law and protected by criminal penalties for unauthorized disclosure. Other such systems protect satellite reconnaisance programs, the military plans for general nuclear war (known as the SIOP), and covert operations of the CIA. It is, of course, impossible to know what others may now exist.

Information in these special systems is often of technical rather than direct political interest. In general it is much less likely to be leaked than information protected only by the general classification system. Because of the overall bias toward secrecy the salient danger is not that information vital to national security will be disclosed, but that politically critical decisions will be made without due consultation—either horizontally or vertically, inside the bureaucracy or in the country at large.

Public Release and Leaks

Our description of the secrecy system has thus far emphasized the incentives for secrecy and the rules that permit much significant information to be kept secret.

From a comparative perspective, one may nonetheless be impressed at how much is made public in the United States. Some people, indeed, argue that nothing of importance can be kept secret. This is a great exaggeration, but it is certainly true that much information does eventually become available.

A great deal is deliberately made public in speeches or press conferences by the President or other high officials, although in some cases the news released at a press conference comes out spontaneously. Information is also released routinely in daily press briefings of the various departments.

Other information is made public in congressional testimony. In a public session a senior official may submit a prepared statement containing something he has consciously decided to make public. On occasion, questions asked in open hearings may lead to spontaneous release of information. When hearings are held in executive session, a declassification process takes place prior to release of the testimony, in which officials of the executive branch delete data that they deem properly classified. Thus the very existence of the MIRV program[9] was considered classified information by those reviewing secret congressional testimony until Secretary of Defense Robert McNamara finally decided to talk about the subject—a decision forced by domestic criticism of the administration's failure to develop important new weapons systems. Thereafter, references to MIRV were permitted to appear in the unclassified versions of congressional testimony.

Information may reach the public less formally by way of background press conferences and interviews held by senior government officials. In some cases these arrangements permit the information to be attributed to "a high official" or a "senior official" of the U.S. government. At other times, the reporter may make the information public only on his own authority, without attributing it to any source.

A reporters's reliance on an anonymous tip by an official, a Congressman, congressional aide or a foreign embassy employee may indicate that the person giving the information does not feel that he has authority to do so, or simply that he wishes to conceal where the leak came from.[10] These tips are often documented by techniques of investigative journalism, with or without further official assistance. Indeed, important stories are sometimes broken in this way with no deliberate assistance from any official. Yet the incentives for secrecy affect the press as well as officials. A powerful tradition of self-censorship has grown up since the Cold War period, when press representatives, like most Americans, accepted the national security rationale as offered in good faith and founded on substantial logic. That tradition continues to play a significant role. Moreover, reporters and publishers are highly dependent on official sources for information and they must hesitate to jeopardize these symbiotic relationships by publishing stories that officials are determined to withhold. Depending on the prevailing climate of opinion, they may be threatened with sanctions ranging anywhere from cancellation of presidential newspaper subscriptions or exclusion from Air Force One all the way up to wiretapping, civil actions, or criminal prosecution.

The continuing willingness of the press, even in the post-Vietnam/Watergate period, to accept official interpretations of the needs of national security was exemplified in the spring of 1975 by an episode involving an unusual CIA project. In order to recover a Soviet submarine that had sunk to the bottom of the Pacific Ocean, the CIA in 1971 contracted secretly with the Howard Hughes-owned Summa Corporation to construct a special salvage vessel, the *Glomar Explorer*. This boat, which masqueraded as a privately owned ship used for deep-sea mining activities, succeeded in raising a portion of the Soviet submarine.[11]

Journalist Seymour Hersh got wind of the story at that time, but he set his inquiry aside to pursue more pressing matters. In 1975, however, papers revealing the secret project were carried off in a robbery of the Summa Corporation office. When the robbers tried to extort hush money, the tense negotiations came to the attention of the *Los Angeles Times*, and soon the underlying secret leaked out. Following the initial, partly erroneous story in the newspaper's early editions, the CIA persuaded the *L. A. Times* to kill the story. Within a short time, Hersh in New York had an accurate account ready for publication, but the *N. Y. Times* management also agreed not to publish it after pleas from CIA Director William Colby. Although the story spread rapidly by word of mouth, the director appealed successfully to each newspaper, news magazine, and network in turn, persuading them that national security required suppression of the story. Finally Jack Anderson broke ranks and revealed the story on the radio, freeing the *New York Times* and the *Washington Post* to print longer accounts, Although no visible damage to national security resulted, intriguing questions were raised about the relationship of the Hughes organization to the CIA. The supersecret vessel has already outlived its usefulness and been retired. The issue of CIA infiltration of the private sector remains to be fully ventilated.

While reporters today can be counted on to go after stories with some determination, and publishers too are willing to go further than they once were, clearly there are limits to what the newspapers will publish. Those restraints are largely determined by the explicit demands and tacit expectations of the government officials who control the information that the press requires.

Officials, particularly lower-level officials, often give information to the press in order to influence the President or other members of the bureacracy whom they cannot reach directly. Most senior officials in Washington regularly read the *New York Times* and the *Washington Post,* as well as one or more news magazines. The way these media present an issue has a strong impact on the political climate. Thus, Pentagon officials concerned about some apparent Soviet military buildup have frequently leaked information in the hope of augmenting high-level concern about the issue. By the same token, an official may withhold information from the press simply because he wishes to keep it from others in the bureaucracy.

Leaks are also frequently used in the struggle for personal prestige. When it became known that Chester Bowles had opposed the Bay of Pigs invasion, it was taken by sophisticated observers as a sign that the Kennedys were angry with him, rather than as an indication that he was in line for a higher position. Obviously, information may directly affect an official's reputation or embarrass him indirectly by implicating him as the apparent source of the leak.[12] The opposite tactic, in which secrecy is used, sometimes under a national security cover, to obscure individual responsibility and protect official reputations, is, of course, a pervasive phenomenon.

Foreign governments are another potential target for the release of national security information. For example, an American negotiating position becomes more credible to foreign leaders when it is shown to have Congressional and public support. Thus during the Vietnam negotiations of the Johnson administration, conciliatory American proposals were often made first unofficially and in secret and then reiterated in a public statement. The secret contact would establish that the proposal was serious and not merely for propaganda effect; the public statement would manifest the President's commitment to the proposal and his ability to carry it out.

When the message secretly conveyed is likely to produce intense opposition and debate in the United States, a public affirmation of it may be more muted. Henry Kissinger, for instance, conveyed threats to the North Vietnamese in 1969 that if they did not settle the conflict quickly the United States would escalate the war. The administration was not able to repeat these explicit threats publicly; the President announced only the warning that "nobody has anything to gain by delay." Meanwhile, Kissinger's private message was covertly but powerfully reinforced by the commencement of bombing in Cambodia.

The important point is that the prevailing system of disclosure, while intrinsically capable both of assisting public debate and of harming the national security, is primarily oriented toward the parochial needs of members of the executive branch. Much information does become public through regular channels or by leaks; yet the criteria for release are determined not by the public interest in informed debate but by the particular interest of those who control the information. These interests may or may not coincide in a given case with those of the public as a whole. In general, little if any information is released because of a belief in the congressional or public right to know and to participate. As a whole, this disclosure system is haphazard, unseemly, and unreliable.[13]

We are convinced that the harms to national security for which leaking is sometimes blamed have been vastly overstated. Certainly we discern no such harms in connection with the examples considered in this study.

It appears that the more significant shortcoming of the disclosure system is its failure to adequately inform legitimately interested parties of decisions and actions pending. Information of no value to foreign governments and of great value to Americans is often kept secret for substantial periods of time, resulting in decisions of inferior quality. Moreover, the secrecy system has severely compromised the integrity of our constitutional decision-making process and had led to serious infringments of the civil liberties of Americans.

While the gravest abuses were perpetrated by individuals no longer on the scene, of course the structural problems we have described were not remedied by Richard Nixon's resignation. Unlike most officials of the executive branch, Congress has come to appreciate these continuing problems and has been groping toward curative reforms. Extensive hearings held in the wake of the Pentagon Papers episode generated various proposals for legislation to ensure more adequate publicity.

Some of these have already become law. Their effect is the subject of the next chapter.

Chapter 4

Recent Efforts at Reform

The congressional forces supporting tighter secrecy in the Cold War period were extremely active in investigating and exposing alleged security risks. As far as legislation was concerned, however, the members of Congress generally felt that the matter should be left to the executive branch. Their involvement was limited to a few measures that had minimal impact on public debate. The general espionage laws, dating back to 1911, were thought to apply only to spying. The several new measures passed in the Cold War era authorized secrecy for specific kinds of information, but their scope was narrow, and they have seldom been the occasion of court proceedings or other controversy.[1]

The heart of the formal secrecy system has been the classification system established by executive order, first in the Truman administration and then as modified by President Eisenhower. Today it is based on Executive Order No. 11652, issued by President Nixon on March 10, 1972. It provides that material whose release might damage the national security is classified top secret, secret, or confidential, according to the degree of damage anticipated.[2] Information may be withheld from release only if its disclosure could, at least, be "reasonably expected" to cause damage to the national security. An implementing directive requires that any substantial doubt be resolved in favor of release.[3]

41

In practice the apparent simplicity of the executive order's three-tiered system is totally undone by the myriad of special procedures and classifications that have grown up with or without proper legal sanction. For example, the categories of "restricted data" (for atomic energy secrets) and "communications intelligence" are authorized by separate congressional legislation. Also in use are several special clearances and a vast number of restrictive distribution designators.[4] As a result, even a very high-ranking official with a top-secret clearance cannot estimate intelligently the degree and significance of his ignorance.

Under executive order the right to classify information has been delegated and redelegated to a very large number of officials in a number of agencies. There now are a substantial number of people—some 17,000—entitled to classify information.

Moreover, under the procedure known as derivative classification, any document that contains information from a document already classified must itself be classified. In addition, the classification procedures require that every page of a bound document be stamped with the classification level of the most sensitive piece of information in the document. Thus, a document containing even a single piece of top secret information would be classified top secret on every page. Any official copying any sentence from that document would be authorized, if not required, to stamp. his entire new document"top secret." While the current procedures do require automatic declassification after a specified number of years, they still permit individual documents to be exempted at the classifying agency's discretion.

This system, as we said above, has permitted and encouraged the withholding of mountains of information from the public. A good deal is of historical or technical interest only, for despite the provisions for "automatic" declassification, much material from World War II and the Cold War period remains classified. More important, the executive order contains no clear mandate for disclosure of any specific kind of information; it does not encourage broad discussion of fundamental issues even within the executive branch, and provides no support for individuals who might wish to bring such an issue before Congress or the public. The classification system has in no way inhibited Presidents and their advisers from proceeding on a secret basis when it comes to major policy decisions and operations.

It is true that the executive order provides no authority for withholding any information from Congress. But classified documents come before that body in a manner that not only precludes effective congressional participation in policy-making but also substantially hinders their oversight of executive compliance with existing legislation.

For years Congress was leery of tampering with this system. Reform proposals were liable to be countered by the executive branch with charges of impracticality and irresponsibility. However self-serving these charges might have been, Congress could not proceed in the absence of powerful and tenacious public support. The Freedom of Information Act passed in 1967 ultimately contained a broad exemption for classified information, and no other reform proposal came close to enactment.

The changed political climate of the 1970's, though, has been far more conducive to affirmative congressional participation on national security affairs. Thus, the years 1972-1974 saw enactment of three selective measures directing the President to consult with Congress about specific kinds of action. In 1974, moreover, Congress amended the Freedom of Information Act to facilitate declassification of national security information. Today any person may request such information and may obtain court review if the executive branch refuses to release it.

These are important innovations; but, as we shall see, they leave the heart of the secrecy system intact.

Mandatory Consultation Requirements

The most significant of the new consultation requirements is established by the 1973 War Powers Resolution, enacted over presidential veto. Section three of this measure directs the President to consult with Congress whenever American forces engage in combat or are in imminent danger of so doing; later sections provide for congressional approval or veto of U.S. combat activity. Section four requires a prompt *and public* report to Congress when the President orders troops into foreign territory or when it is clear that combat is imminent.[5]

So far the report procedures of section four have been used on four occasions, in connection with the evacuations from Vietnam and Cambodia and with the Mayaguez affair. Each of these episodes passed so quickly that by the time the report was submitted, the operation was already completed.

The only instance predictably involving significant combat activity, thereby triggering the prior consultation requirement of section three, was the Mayaguez affair. As subsequent hearings brought out, President Ford took an extremely conservative view of his duty to "consult" on this occasion. After the Cambodian government seized an American merchant ship, the President met twice with the National Security Council over a two-day period. Then he had members of his staff contact selected congressional leaders and inform them that he had decided in principle to use force to recapture the ship. The next day, the Senate Foreign Relations Committee received a secret briefing from the President, immediately prior to his issuance of the actual orders for the assault. Only after the fighting ended that same day was the affair made public.[6]

This limited and hopefully atypical experience with the War Powers Resolution suggests that it makes a great difference whether public notice is given *before the fact*. Prior consultation with Congress is apt to be more significant if Congress must develop a response in public.

Questions of timing aside, it is a great merit of the bill that section four reports are required to be made public. The resolution thus outlaws the kind of protracted secret warfare that was conducted in Laos and Cambodia. Moreover, by calling for a public report as soon as the President knows combat is imminent, it helps to deter secret moves that might lead to the outbreak of war.

A second policy area in which Congress has moved to increase its influence is the transfer of military equipment abroad. For many years Congress annually appropriated a lump sum for military assistance, without public disclosure of the equipment or countries for which funds were earmarked. That information was supplied to Congress on a secret basis. When Senator William Proxmire became chairman of the relevant appropriations subcommittee, he recognized that without public support he could not convince his colleagues to accept the cutbacks that he desired. Proxmire therefore announced that he would not report out an appropriation bill unless the specifics were made public. The State Department objected that publicity would embarrass other governments, who might wish to conceal how much or how little aid they were getting, but Proxmire stood firm.

Release of the figures did not lead any country to withdraw from the program. Congress found, however, that it still had no control over actual weapons transfers, because the information that had been supplied was regarded by the administation as tentative rather than binding. Thus, in 1973 Congress directed the President to provide advance notice of all sales exceeding $25 million.[7]

A serious shortcoming of that measure was that it permitted the required notification to be made in secret. Many proposed sales were, in fact, kept secret, which has greatly blunted the impact of the amendment. The covert assistance to the forces in Angola went forward despite secret briefings of congressional committees. In contrast, public notice of a proposed sale of missiles to Jordan in August 1975 led to rejection of the request. In 1976 Congress added a provision to the Military Assistance Act that requires public notice of all proposed sales while permitting some details to remain secret.[8].

Executive agreements have been subject to similar changes in treatment. Prior to 1972 there was no obligation on the part of the President to inform the Congress, publicly or in secret, of their existence. Important agreements that were kept secret included one in 1969 with Spain that could have been construed as a security commitment, and the promise by President Nixon to South Vietnamese President Thieu that the United States would respond "with full force" to a violation of the Vietnam cease-fire agreement.[9]

Since 1972 the Church Amendment has required that all executive agreements be disclosed to Congress, but even that provision has several loopholes. First, it is limited to documents actually signed by both parties. More important, it permits the notification to be made in secret whenever the administration determines that the text of the agreement—or even its existence—should not be made public.[10] Liberal use has been made of this loophole, as administrations have chosen to keep from the public most of the agreements disclosed to Congress under the Church Amendment.

In August 1975 Congressman Les Aspin complained that this procedure prevented any effective congressional oversight of executive agreements, and he urged the President to make public at least an unclassified summary of each one. A few months later, the Senate Foreign Relations Committee insisted that all agreements and commitments made in connection with the interim Egyptian-Israeli settlement be made public before it would approve the dispatch of American technicians to the Sinai. The committee emphasized that any assurances kept secret would be regarded by Congress as null and void.

Important lessons can be drawn from these recent attempts at reform. As Congress has moved to assert its control in specific policy areas, it has come to appreciate the importance of requiring public disclosure of critical information, so that public support can be marshalled for the measures Congress deems necessary. It has learned how to use its powers, fiscal and otherwise, to compel such disclosure despite executive branch resistance, gaining confidence in doing so as the threatened disasters for national security failed to materialize. Congress knows that responsibility for reconciling the imperatives of national security and constitutional procedures does not rest with the Chief Executive alone; it too has an important and constructive role to play.

Specific, substantive legislated guidelines have emerged as an important tool for that purpose. Laws authorizing secrecy have been found appropriate for information that is of great value to potential enemies and of minimal value to public policy debate. Mandatory disclosure requirements are equally suited for certain information that Congress needs on a public basis, but that tends to be withheld for inappropriate reasons.

Specific disclosure requirements must be complemented by

effective procedures for obtaining the release of other documents that may be wanted from time to time. Congress has recently taken steps in this direction as well.

The Freedom of Information Act

Prior to the passage of the Freedom of Information Act in 1967, there existed no legal right on the part of the press or the public to demand access to the files of the U.S. government. The courts had not been prepared to hold that the Constitution, and in particular the First Amendment, itself created such a right; only in a few special cases had Congress created a statutory right to demand information. Thus, government agencies of all kinds regularly and casually rejected requests for information, and citizens had no recourse except to seek the aid of their representatives in Congress. Over a period of years the House Government Operations Subcommittee on Information held a series of hearings detailing the road blocks that government had put in the way of the release of information. These hearings led to the first Freedom of Information Act.

Under the provisions of this act still in effect, government agencies are routinely required to release certain information involving their rules, regulations, and organizational procedures. Any other information in an agency's possession can be requested. Agencies could refuse to release information if it fit into one of nine specified exemptions, including matters "specifically required by Executive Order to be kept secret in the interest of national defense or foreign policy."

The exemption for national defense and foreign policy information received very little attention during the hearings and debate on the act. Opposition to the whole idea of a Freedom of Information Act was universal within the executive branch, and since abuses in the secrecy system had not yet come to light, public concern was minimal. To avoid a threatened presidential veto, Congress took pains to adopt a gingerly approach to national security information. By defining such information in terms of the fact of classification, they ratified the wide discretion already enjoyed by the executive branch.

On the whole, the impact of the Freedom of Information Act

was limited, as had been anticipated, to the domestic area. Few requests were made for national defense information, and those were routinely turned aside until some members of Congress made a determined effort to secure information relating to the environmental impact of a planned atomic test to be conducted in Alaska. This controversy produced a definitive Supreme Court interpretation of the national security exemption in the 1967 Act.

In *Environmental Protection Agency* v. *Mink,*[11] the Court held that the exemption meant whatever the executive branch said it meant: Congress had not intended that the courts review the propriety of particular classifications under the executive order; even where a decision appeared to be "cynical, myopic, or even corrupt," the courts must respect it and exempt the document from disclosure under the Act. However, the Court went on,

> Congress could certainly have provided that the Executive Branch adopt new procedures or it could have established its own procedures—subject only to whatever limitations the Executive privilege may be held to impose upon such congressional ordering.

The 1974 Amendments

The release of the Pentagon Papers in June 1972 triggered a series of hearings, first in the House subcommittee that had reported out the Freedom of Information Act and later in a group of Senate committees concerned with freedom of information, classification, and executive privilege.[12] These hearings probed deeply into the secrecy system, and produced reports that emphasized the abuses of the system and the need for changes. Many members, convinced that much of the information in the Pentagon Papers should have been released, now recommended amendments to overrule the *Mink* decision. These would allow individuals to request the release of classified information and authorize courts to review the propriety of its classification.[13]

In 1974 Congress enacted major revisions to the Freedom of Information Act, including a number of procedural changes. For example, any request that "reasonably describes" a record in an agency's possession obliges the agency to review that record and determine whether the information is currently properly classified. Segregable portions of a document that are not exempt must be made public, even if other portions are still properly withheld. The new act tightens certain provisions that had allowed both undue delays and excessive fees under the 1967 law; most important is the new amendment requiring an initial agency response within ten days. Finally, tough administrative sanctions are prescribed where the court determines that information was arbitrarily and capriciously withheld. These changes certainly add up to a substantial reform.

Exemptions for national security information and for investigatory files, which had been given particularly expansive application by the courts, were also radically changed. (The other exemptions were left as they had been in the original act.)[14]

As it was finally approved by Congress, the new (b) (1) exemption says that materials can be withheld for national security reasons only if they are:

a) specifically authorized under criteria established by executive order to be kept secret in the interests of national defense and foreign policy, and
b) are in fact properly classified pursuant to such executive order.

The Conference Report noted that "both procedural and substantive criteria contained in the relevant executive order must be followed." Under existing criteria, information may be withheld from the public if the classifying official has no substantial doubt that disclosure could reasonably be expected to cause damage to the national security.[15]

The court's mandate under the new act is simply to determine independently whether secrecy is warranted by these criteria; the substantive standards of the executive order are adopted without change. However, in an unsuccessful effort to ward off a threatened veto by President Gerald Ford, the conference committee later inserted some softening remarks into its report:

In *Environmental Protection Agency* v. *Mink, et al.*, 410 U.S. 73 (1973), the Supreme Court ruled that *in camera* inspection of documents withheld under section 552(b)(1) of the law, authorizing the withholding of classified information, would ordinarily be precluded in Freedom of Information cases, unless Congress directed otherwise. H.F. 12471 amends the present law to permit such *in camera* examination at the discretion of the court. While *in camera* examination need not be automatic, in many situations it will plainly be necessary and appropriate. Before the court orders *in camera* inspection, the Government should be given the opportunity to establish by means of testimony or detailed affidavits that the documents are clearly exempt from disclosure. The burden remains on the Government under this law.

However, the conferees recognize that the Executive departments responsible for national defense and foreign policy matters have unique insights into what adverse effects might occur as a result of public disclosure of a particular classified record. Accordingly, the conferees expect that the Federal Courts, in making *de novo* determinations in section 552(b)(1) cases under the Freedom of Information law, will accord substantial weight to an agency's affidavit concerning the details of the classified status of the disputed record.[16]

Despite this reassuring language, and despite the overwhelming approval of the act by both houses of Congress, President Ford vetoed the bill.[17] In doing so, he paid particular attention to the change in the (b)(1) exemption, charging that the provision for *de novo* judicial review was unconstitutional. Congress obviously was not persuaded, for it overrode the President's veto.[18]

The amendments went into effect on February 19, 1974, and as a result of requests and lawsuits under the FOIA, many documents that had previously been withheld have been released. These include International Red Cross reports on POWs in Vietnam, portions of the negotiating volumes of the Pentagon Papers, a report on CIA domestic activities prepared for President Ford, various executive branch studies of the intelligence community, and summaries of the private files of J. Edgar Hoover.[19]

However, it remains unclear whether the act's impact will be as extensive as was intended. For one thing, government agencies can attempt to use other exemptions of the Freedom of Information Act to deny the release of information relating to national defense and foreign policy. The most significant of these are exemptions (b)(3), relating to information "specifically authorized by legislation to be kept secret" and exemption (b)(5), relating to inter- and intra- agency memoranda.

The (b)(3) exemption clearly applies to the atomic, cryptographic, and CIA personnel information covered by special secrecy legislation.[20] Moreover, the CIA claims that the Director's authority[21] to protect "intelligence sources and methods" is a "specific authority" to keep secret under (b)(3) any information that the Director deems to be related to that responsibility. The Court of Appeals for the D.C Circuit ruled[22] in November 1976 that both statutes did authorize withholding but held that both statutes should be narrowly construed and limited to information on CIA personnel, and documents whose release could reasonably be expected to cause injury by revealing intelligence sources and methods.

Exemption (b)(5) extends only to advice and facts that are 'inexorably intertwined" with advice, and does not apply to other factual information contained in an advice memorandum. Despite these limitations, the executive branch can rely heavily on the advice privilege in order to withhold national security information. It can claim that the manner of presenting facts is itself an aspect of advice, and that in any case all the national security information in the document is "inexorably intertwined" with advice.

Far more significant than these potential loopholes is the fact that the new act still does not require the executive branch to balance the public's need for the information against the possible harm to national security, nor does it permit the courts to weigh these considerations. Any information that in the court's view meets the existing criteria for "confidential" classification thus remains exempt from disclosure. Congress was quite realistic in "expecting" the courts to give "substantial weight" to the classifying agency's own determination. Among the types of information the courts have refused to release are the CIA budget, documents related to CIA invasions of Cuba, to CIA covert operations in the late 1940s and early 1950s, and portions of the CIA charter.[23]

Surely the present law is not immune to criticism, and its impact will depend on the vigor of the public in requesting information as well as the judicial resolution of legal ambiguities. Yet it seems clear that a formal disclosure process involving independent review is a major advance from the chaotic and unprincipled system of leaks and counterleaks we described in the last chapter.

Classification Legislation

These reforms are steps in the right direction, and they have somewhat improved the flow of vital information to Congress and the public. Yet the specific congressional consultation requirements are narrow in scope and do not always require the public disclosure necessary to make that consultation meaningful. Under the Freedom of Information Act, moreover, the courts remain bound to implement the overbroad secrecy guidelines laid down by executive order. Congress has therefore begun to consider the desirability of legislating a balanced and comprehensive new classification system.

During the Ninety-third Congress (ending in 1974) congressional committees held extensive hearings on a number of proposals[24] whose basic object was to eliminate the "abuses" that afflict the present system. The main thrust of reform, therefore, involved limiting the number of officials who could classify, and requiring more speedy and more automatic declassification of secret information. The limitations of this approach became clear as Congress evaluated the impact of similar reforms introduced by President Nixon.

The Nixon order had already drastically reduced the number of officials who could classify material "top secret" and had somewhat reduced the number of classifiers overall. Nevertheless there was minimal effect on the flow of current information to the public, since release is blocked as effectively by the lowest classfication marking as by the highest. In fact, even the incidence of "top secret" classifications did not decline as expected, because of the principle of "derivative classification": While a given official may have no authority himself to classify information "top secret," he can and will so classify any document containing information that someone else has classified in that way.

Another change imposed by the new Nixon order was the tightening of the system for automatic declassification. In principle, most information would now be automatically downgraded and declassified according to a fixed schedule. In practice, most significant information is exempt from the schedule, because it relates to a "specific foreign relations matter the continuing protection of which is essential to the national security."[25] Moreover, the disclosure of documents years after they were written, while of great interest to historians, does not serve the interest in public debate on issues of immediate concern.

Perhaps the most promising change introduced by the Nixon order was to alter the definition of what could be classified "confidential" from information whose release "*could cause injury*" to information whose release "*could reasonably be expected to cause injury.*" This straightforward attempt to tighten the threshhold standard for secrecy had no visible effect. Senior officials of the executive branch do not even appear to be aware of the change.[26] Junior officials who know about the reform are unlikely to feel that it requires the release of information they wish to keep secret.

The failure of the much heralded Nixon executive order to make any real difference blunted the appeal of the similar legislative proposals brought forward in the Ninety-third Congress, and these were not reintroduced in the Ninety-fourth. Despite the congressional concern about national security secrecy, Congress did little work on the problem in 1975-1976. Partly this was due to preoccupation with other issues; but there was also great uncertainty about what should be done.

We think it is clear that the problem is not "abuses" of the classification system but rather its lack of salience for senior members of the executive branch and its failure to give explicit weight to the value of public debate on major issues. For senior and junior officials alike, the classification system has failed to supply any serious incentive to consider the value of such debate; instead partisan and bureaucratic calculations have played a disproportionate role in secrecy decisions. The Freedom of Information Act has now introduced a mechanism for more impartial review; but the controlling guidelines are still those of the executive secrecy system itself.

Chapter 5

Toward a More Open System

The new classification system we propose for the executive branch has several novel elements, not least of which is that it would be established by legislation rather than by executive order.

Some may argue that the President can judge better than Congress how far reform should go. But we believe it is unrealistic to expect any President to carry out truly effective reform, since it would mean the restriction of his own freedom of action. Nor is it realistic to suppose that Presidents can, with the best of will, abolish by executive order the bureaucratic penchant for secrecy. It is very clear that uncontrolled executive discretion is central to the disease, and the curtailment of that discretion must be part of any cure. Where the law sanctifies unbridled discretion, or where its standards are ambiguous and loosely drawn, officials will feel justified in interpreting the law in a manner that conforms to their own political or bureaucratic interest.

If this is true for rules laid down by Congress or the judiciary, it is even more true for executive orders, such as the one that now authorizes the classification system. The diffusion through the bureaucracy of a rather casual attitude has been abetted by the conduct of Presidents and their immediate associates, who have tended to act as if the guidelines and procedures of the classification system were not to be taken too literally, at least by the upper echelons.

We believe that this attitude can be corrected by the establishment of clear, specific, and authoritative legal norms, and that most officials will try conscientiously to obey an explicit duty of disclosure, established and supervised by the coordinate branches of government and supported by public opinion.

The case for programmatic, regulatory legislation would have made little sense before the modern period. As we have pointed out, until recently there was no bureaucratic dimension to the secrecy issue, which was typically discussed in the context of direct and essentially partisan confrontations between a President and his congressional opposition. In these episodes the contestants quite naturally found that political struggle and appeals to public opinion were the appropriate way to pursue disputes over information. They were interested not in long-range institutional solutions but in winning the immediate foreign policy and electoral battle.

It is the more complex institutional character of the modern problem that makes programmatic legislative action uniquely appropriate. With hindsight we can more fully appreciate that neither the good character of officials nor the electoral accountability of Presidents is enough to secure voluntary and adequate publicity. The cynical practices of "public relations" and "news management" have undermined public trust, and leaks have not proved a reliable or edifying alternative. At times, the viability of the constitutional system has been brought into question.[1]

We do not deny that the traditional political controls still have a role to play. When confrontation rises to the most acute levels, the impeachment power may become relevant. Short of this, Congress may seek to compel disclosure of particular information by using the power of the purse or other techniques of a political nature.

These techniques may succeed in particular cases, but they cannot be used too often, and they are not capable of producing lasting changes in the way major policy decisions are made. That goal requires a substantial restructuring of the secrecy system itself.

There are good reasons why this task cannot safely be entrusted to the executive branch. Constitutionally, the establishment of criteria and procedures regulating the classification of information is a proper legislative function, though Congress has until now delegated that responsibility to the President. We think the time has come for Congress to reclaim it.

Legislated reform, we believe, is a constitutionally appropriate and a politically viable approach. In fact, no satisfactory alternative is available. Nevertheless, we recognize that complex political and administrative problems do not magically disappear with the promulgation of a formal regulation. Indeed, we are sensitive to the objection that legislation might succeed only in strengthening the status quo.

It would certainly be most unfortunate if Congress enacted legislation that seemed to ratify the extremely broad discretion now claimed by the executive branch. So far Congress has shown no disposition to do so, but no other approach has gained substantial support. We think the answer lies in an extension of the technique that Congress has used successfully, but unsystematically in the past: the enactment of clear, specific, and balanced criteria for disclosure and for secrecy.

Our proposed system would assign information to one of three broad categories: (1) automatically released, (2) presumptively classified, and (3) requiring the exercise of discretion, with explicit consideration of the information's value for enlightened public debate. Decisions to keep information secret would be subject to independent scrutiny, both within the executive branch and by the courts. The principles behind our three broad categories of information can be succinctly stated:

Information necessary to congressional exercise of its constitutional powers to declare war, to raise armies, to regulate the armed forces, to ratify treaties, and to approve official appointments must be made available not only to Congress but to the public. [2]

Because we do not feel that this principle meets the criterion of specificity required for effective control, we propose the legislation of specific categories of information that should routinely be made public. Experience and common sense, we believe, provide reliable criteria for anticipating the kinds of decisions that fall into this category; and those criteria should be enacted into law. Specifically, we would include information relating to: (a) Americans engaged in combat or in imminent prospect of combat; (b) American forces abroad; (c) nuclear weapons abroad; (d) financing of foreign operations or foreign military forces; (e) commitments to do (a)—(d) or commencement of negotiations contemplating such commitments; (f) intelligence organizations: existence, budgets, and functions; (g) weapons systems: concepts and costs; and (h) actions in violation of law.

It is our judgment that Congress may confidently require this information to be released, without fear of serious injury to the national defense. Beyond any doubt, the constitutional case for making this information public outweighs any harm that might result.

For a few narrow categories of information, mostly technical, public disclosure does not appear useful for policy debate. It could, however, be expected to give substantial assistance to potential adversaries. Such information, though it should be available to Congress on a secret basis, is entitled to a heavy presumption against public disclosure.[3]. Specifically, we refer to (a) weapons systems: details of advanced system design and operational characteristics; (b) details of plans for military operations; (c) details of ongoing diplomatic negotiations; and (d) intelligence methods: codes, technology, and identity of spies.

Information not in these clear-cut categories should be made public unless a reasoned judgment is made that the probable costs to national security clearly outweigh the value of the information for public debate; and that judgment should be subject to independent review.

Automatic Release

Americans engaged in combat or in imminent prospect of combat. Congress's powers to declare war, to raise funds for and to regulate the armed forces are of little practical significance if the President can order armed forces into combat without even informing Congress. The Founding Fathers were of course aware of the military value of surprise attack; yet they deliberately deprived the' President of power to take such action, because of its implications for liberty at home. As the Cambodia bombing case illustrates, Presidents have recently circumvented constitutional procedures by authorizing protracted secret combat operations. In response, Congress has already legislated a narrow requirement for public disclosure in the War Powers Bill.

We see little risk to national security from our proposal to strengthen this requirement; certainly an enemy or potential enemy will ordinarily be aware that American forces are engaged in combat against them or are in a combat zone. In any case, we believe that the implications of combat activity create a paramount public interest in disclosure.

The designation of military personnel as "advisors" would not avoid a well-drafted disclosure requirement, since the forces would be in imminent danger of coming under hostile fire. Nor should the President be permitted to conduct such operations in secret simply by utilizing civilian employees of the United States government or foreign mercenaries. The requirement for disclosure should apply whenever the United States is paying the salaries of those engaged in combat.

Only the fact of combat or introduction of forces would have to be made public. Details of combat plans and operations could be kept secret.[4]

American forces abroad. Congress's power to declare war and the public's right to debate questions of war and peace can also be vitiated by the peacetime stationing of American forces on the front line, where they will inevitably be drawn into combat if a war should start. The only reason for taking such measures in secret would be to avoid domestic criticism; obviously, the arrival of American forces will not long remain secret in the area where they are stationed. The deployment and redeployment of American troops overseas should be subject, in general terms, to timely congressional and public discussion.

Nuclear weapons abroad. The logic of a requirement to report that American forces are stationed in a particular country would not extend to a public listing of all their military equipment. However, we propose that the President be required to report publicly the countries in which the United States stores nuclear weapons.

Nuclear weapons are qualitatively different from other armaments. Their use anywhere would injure humanity in profound and lasting ways. The presence of nuclear weapons in a particular country not only implies that they might be used in its defense; it also creates a risk of their unauthorized use by the host government, or of their seizure by domestic dissidents or invading forces.

At present, the executive branch admits publicly that it stores more than 7,000 nuclear weapons in Europe, but declines to identify publicly the European countries in which weapons are kept. In 1975 Secretary of Defense James Schlesinger stated that nuclear weapons are stored in Korea but the executive still refuses to indicate if nuclear weapons are stored elsewhere. Senator Stuart Symington has, at congressional hearings, indicated that American nuclear weapons are maintained in Greece, Turkey, Korea, and other countries.[5]

Since the United States keeps nuclear weapons in special storage facilities, their presence in a foreign country is seldom, if ever, a secret from Soviet satellite reconnaissance. Secrecy on this question seems designed to avoid public debate in the host countries as well as the United States—a rationale reminiscent of the Cambodia bombing case. Such motives as these are simply not sufficient to offset the need for congressional and public debate on the issues involved.

Financing of foreign combat operations or foreign military forces. The United States transfers military equipment to foreign governments in a variety of ways, including the military assistance program (which can also include transfers of funds to finance combat operations) and foreign military sales programs.

Congress now requires the President to make public the budget figures for intended military assistance grants to particular countries and to provide advance public notice of all proposed sales of military equipment.[6] The executive branch met a previous requirement that permitted secret notice by providing much of the data, including descriptions of the equipment, in secret. Military assistance can be a prelude to the use of American forces. For this reason alone, a requirement of public release seems appropriate. Moreover, it is difficult to see how such disclosure would harm national security. The ability of recipient governments to keep the secret is often quite limited, and potential enemies are likely to be well aware of American involvement. Indeed, for prestige or deterrence the recipient nation often deliberately makes public its military gifts from the United States.

The provision of covert assistance to insurgent or irregular forces is a distinct problem, insofar as such programs could not ordinarily be conducted in the open. The debate over these activities is not, properly speaking, about their secrecy, but about whether they should be engaged in at all.

Commitments to do any of the above; commencement of negotiations contemplating such commitments. The Constitution appears to require that the Senate consent to all international commitments, but in modern times, Presidents have increasingly made use of "executive agreements" to circumvent that formality. While this procedure may be appropriate in some cases, that would not be true in the case of commitments that could lead to combat activity or other consequences equally grave.

Part of the appeal for a President of such informal commitments is that, when the time comes to honor them, Congress may feel bound to stand behind the President's pledge; if not, the United States is legally off the hook, and any charges of bad faith can be leveled at Congress rather than the President. The drawbacks of this technique were underlined by the controversy over aid to South Vietnam in the spring of 1975. The South Vietnamese plea for military assistance to avert the fall of Saigon was bolstered by disclosures that, in conjunction with the agreement signed at the Paris talks in 1972, President Nixon had promised Thieu that the

United States would respond "with full force" to violations of a ceasefire by Hanoi. The Ford administration was legally and politically in no position to send troops or resume bombing in Vietnam; it did not ask Congress for authority to do so. While pointing to congressional resistance in explanation of his apparent failure to honor the commitment, the President urged Congress to keep faith with Saigon by approving a request for massive weapons assistance. Congress refused, raising questions about the value of solemn guarantees from a President of the United States. A timely coordination with Congress concerning the existence and interpretation of this commitment would have mitigated the severe embarrassment occasioned by the episode.

Congress in 1972 required that it be informed of all executive agreements. However, the existing legislation[7] permits agreements to be kept secret from the public whenever the executive so prescribes. We believe that the arguments for public debate on actual combat activity apply with equal force at the time of commitments to engage in combat; the same reasoning applies to commitments to engage in other conduct covered by our mandatory disclosure categories. The President and Congress should not keep such agreements secret because they could not properly carry them out in secret.

If public debate is to be meaningful, it must be timely. Before the United States undertakes a combat commitment, an agreement to station troops abroad, or to supply military aid, the prospect of the agreement should be made public. We think a good way to assure adequate ventilation of the issues is by promptly announcing the commencement of the negotiations and their general subject matter.

Indeed, the general tenor of the American negotiating position could often safely be made public as well, but we are not prepared to recommend that this be required in all cases.

Intelligence organizations: existence, budgets and functions. Secret operations are anathema to a democracy. They should be permitted, if at all, only in the most compelling circumstances. Yet the United States now has intelligence organizations whose very existence is kept secret (National Reconnaissance Office), whose budget is not made public (Central Intelligence Agency), and whose full range of functions is not known (NRO, CIA, and National Security Agency.)[8]

Our proposal would require that enough information be made public to permit Congress and the public to decide whether the organizations should exist, what functions they should perform, and how much they should spend.

The Constitution seems to require that budgets be made public. Article I, Section 9 states that:

> No money shall be drawn from the Treasury, but in consequence of appropriations made by law. and a regular statement and account of the receipts and expenditures of all public money shall be published from time to time.

National security does not appear to require that the overall budgets of these agencies be kept secret. Former CIA director William Colby has conceded, for example, that making public the overall intelligence budget would not injure national security, although he opposed release of the figure on the grounds that it would generate pressure to release additional data.[9]

Congress authorized the creation of the CIA and defined its functions in very general terms. It is clear that Congress believed it was creating an intelligence evaluation organization, and not an agency that would conduct covert operations abroad or intelligence operations in the United States.[10] These latter functions are purportedly authorized by secret directives issued by the executive from time to time. The National Security Agency was created by a secret presidential directive; it is not known by what means the National Reconnaissance Office was created. There does not appear to be any justification for creating organizations in secret or keeping their functions secret. The Constitution requires congressional authority for creation of executive agencies, as well as congressional oversight of their conduct. But the willingness of Congress to delegate these functions to the President has, until recently, vitiated those responsibilities. In 1975 there were numerous disclosures about the range of the CIA's covert operations abroad, and CIA Director William Colby detailed the agency's domestic activities. These disclosures have permitted an unprecedented and welcome public debate on the principles involved. Similarly, it is well known that a Pentagon agency conducts satellite reconnaissance and that the NSA monitors electronic signals and attempts to break codes. No harm would result from admitting this publicly.

Weapons systems: concepts and costs. Once a weapons system has been developed and is ready for production, it may be too late to decide not to deploy it. Often billions have already been spent, and enormous bureaucratic and industrial momentum has built up behind the program. Effective congressional and public control requires discussion of *proposed* new programs.

For example, the fact that the United States was developing MIRVs (multiple warheads) for its strategic missiles was kept secret for many years, precluding public debate on what many consider to be an undesirable escalation of the arms race. By the time the program was made public in 1967, it was too late for opponents to build the public constituency necessary to stop its development.

Public disclosure would involve the general outline of the proposed development and the estimated cost of the system—not its technical detail. Such limited disclosure, it is true, might have the effect of alerting a potential enemy to our new system, allowing him to copy or neutralize it sooner than might otherwise have occurred.[11] Yet disclosure may be equally conducive to mutual agreements not to develop the proposed system, and in any case we think the benefits of a temporary strategic advantage are more than offset by the destabilizing effects of attempts to exploit such a situation. The potential costs of disclosure thus are far outweighed by the clear gains of permitting public debate on such large expenditures of public funds.

Actions in violation of law. It is of course unrealistic to ask the President to supply Congress with a list of illegal actions he is undertaking. However, it would not be inappropriate to place an obligation upon any official of the executive branch who learns of unlawful activities to make the information public. For example, under an amendment to the Foreign Assistance Act passed in 1974, Congress prohibited the conduct of covert operations in foreign countries "other than those intended solely for obtaining intelligence," unless the President approved the operation and reported the fact of such operations to the appropriate committees of Congress.[12] An official learning of a covert operation designed for a purpose other than intelligence, which had not been approved by the President or reported to Congress, would be obligated to make the information public.

The categories listed above represent an attempt to specify the most critical types of information needed by Congress and the public in order to participate intelligently in vital decisions on foreign policy and national defense. Upon examination, it appears certain that the release of these kinds of information would not have any serious detrimental impact on national security. It is rarely possible—or even advantageous—to conceal such information from potential enemies. In the past, as we have shown, the secrecy system has largely operated with reference to domestic audiences. Any adverse effects of increased disclosure to foreign governments will be far outweighed by the value of having this information available to Congress and the public.

Presumptive Secrecy

In addition to legislating categories for mandatory disclosure, Congress should designate certain kinds of information as presumptively secret, because they are not in general important for public debate, while their release could have detrimental effects on national security. This information should, however, be available to Congress on a secret basis; and in any particular case the presumption of secrecy might be overcome if responsible officials are satisfied that there is a strong need for the information for public debate on a major issue.[13]

Categories of sensitive information that should be presumptively secret because of their limited use to the public include the following:[14]

Weapons systems: details of advanced weapons systems design and operational characteristics. One category of such information is already required to be kept secret by the Atomic Energy Act, which specifies that information useful in the manufacture of atomic weapons and other atomic explosive devices should be classified as "restricted data."

Technical characteristics of many nonnuclear weapons systems are quite sensibly kept secret. Secrecy makes it harder for other countries to manufacture these weapons, to counteract them, or to exploit their vulnerabilities. Such secrecy need not interfere with the necessary public debate on appropriations measures, provided that enough information is disclosed to establish the cost and the benefits of the system.[15] Likewise, secrecy need not and should not interfere with appropriate public participation in the effort to institute arms control agreements. Like other strategic issues, arms control proposals involve a complex mixture of technical and political questions. While official experts inevitably play a leading role, their progress should not be entirely insulated from public evaluation.

Details of plans for military operations. Our scheme would require the United States to reveal that it was engaging, or about to engage, in military operations against another country. But the public and Congress need not know the precise operational details in order to debate the wisdom of planned or current operations. Such information could be of great value to a potential opponent.

Ongoing diplomatic negotiations. Diplomatic negotiations cannot, in many cases, be carried on successfully if one or both countries continuously make public the negotiating positions of both sides. Public negotiations very quickly turn into propoganda sessions; the real negotiations, if they survive, occur quietly behind the facade of the formal ones, as in the 1968-1972 Vietnam peace negotiations in Paris. On the other hand, the Pentagon Papers episode illustrates that the competence and sincerity of the negotiating performance of American officials may be a legitimate public concern. While the fact of negotiations should be announced, the positions put forward in the negotiations may properly be kept secret during the period when the negotiations are under way. The door should be left open, however, for a subsequent public evaluation of the transaction.

Intelligence methods: codes, technology, and spies. Specific details of American information gathering activities should be kept secret. That the United States manufactures codes for use in its diplomatic and military operations is, of course, no secret. The United States government officially denies its interception of messages and its attempts to break codes. This "secret" would be a casualty of our scheme, in that the functions of the National Security Agency would have to be made public. There is, however, no reason why the details of the manufacture of codes, the procedures used to break codes, or the fact that any particular code has been broken should be made public.

We have discussed the need for such disclosures about intelligence gathering organizations as will enable the expenditure of public funds to be evaluated and controlled. There is no need for the public or Congress to know the precise operational details of such programs as satellite reconnaissance or foreign governmental communications interception. The latter information is presently protected by statutes against unauthorized disclosure.

The identity of particular spies, or other information compromising to ongoing lawful operations, would of course be appropriate matter for secrecy as well.

The Middle Category: Balancing

These efforts to specify categories of information that must be released and those that should be kept secret do not pretend to cover entirely the field of national security information. Much information will fall, properly so, into a middle category requiring case-by-case judgment. In such cases, the balancing of the value of disclosure to the public, as against the possible harm to the defense or foreign policy of the United States, is left initially to the classifying official. Weighing these factors should proceed on the principle that release is required unless one can reasonably judge that the probable costs to national security clearly outweigh the value of the information for public debate.

Pragmatic Objections:
The Proposed System in Operation

There can be little disagreement, we think, with the ultimate aim of our proposals: to enhance the quality of public debate and of the resulting policies, while at the same time providing due protection for legitimate secrets. It remains to demonstrate that the proposals are well-designed to accomplish this aim—that in practice there would be neither far too much disclosure nor far too little. To show this, we must be more specific about the way our proposed classification system would actually operate.

The proposal to require automatic disclosure of certain categories of information is certain to be criticized for its rigidity. Yet, in our view, this rigidity is an essential requirement. History shows that executive secrecy is not adequately controlled by means of internal self-discipline. Mandatory legislation, we think, is the only promising alternative. The War Powers Act already requires public reporting of U.S. combat activities, and other legislation requires public disclosure of arms transfers. Our proposals constitute a selective extension of this approach, calculated to guarantee that there will be timely public debate on issues of primary importance. The identification of those issues and the initiation of debate cannot safely be left to official discretion. It is appropriate and essential that Congress designate in advance the kinds of information whose release is both of great public value and safe in security terms.

Our mandatory disclosure categories are intended to ensure

that certain decisions vitally and directly affecting the general welfare will be made in a constitutionally acceptable manner. Without question, Congress has the right and the responsibility to participate in basic decisions affecting war and peace, to regulate public spending, and to oversee the activities of the executive branch. The attempt to perform these functions through informal and voluntary cooperation may have succeeded in happier times; in our time it has conspicuously failed.

In the postwar period, many things were done in secret that under our proposals would have had to be disclosed. In some cases disclosure might have made little immediate difference. For example, many of the covert interventions in various countries before the Bay of Pigs could perhaps have been performed openly, without major military risk or domestic opposition. In any case, we think public debate on the appropriateness of such operations would have been highly beneficial.

With respect to the course of events in Indochina, the impact of full disclosure would probably have been far more significant, because our operations there were more controversial and were extended over longer periods of time. If some of the critical information in the Pentagon Papers had been public from the beginning, U.S. involvement might never have reached the point of actual combat. On the other hand, it is possible that the public would have continued to support administration policy indefinitely if not for the emergence of the "credibility gap." Of two things we are certain. First, the disclosures required by our proposals would not have given foreign governments any significant information they did not already have. Second, secrecy was a crucial factor in the loss of trust between the government and the public that developed in this period. That development was far more costly to our society than any damage that public debate could possibly have done.

Without the gift of prophecy, there is no way to prove absolutely that our proposals will never have any adverse effect on the national security. We would point out, however, that the most important restraint on presidential power is one that Congress has already seen fit to impose, in the form of the War Powers

Resolution. That measure, and the related reforms discussed in Chapter 4, have contributed to a somewhat more open style in executive decision-making, without noticeable harm to the national security. In fact, the Mayaguez and Angola episodes illustrate that the presidency has retained an ample, and indeed a dangerous, degree of the "flexibility" that crises are said to demand. The reforms of recent years do not go far enough; our proposals are a measured extension.

We would not recommend extending this approach to cover the entire domain of information that is not presumptively secret, for the costs of such wholesale disclosure would almost surely outweigh the benefits. Yet it is possible that a few additional mandatory disclosure categories could be justified. Our proposals focus on the problem of secret warmaking, brought so sharply to public attention by events of the last decade. Perhaps other, less obvious kinds of issues deserve equal priority. One advantage of the legislative process is the opportunity it affords for careful consideration of aspects of an issue that may have been overlooked at first. That is precisely why we favor a legislated solution.

The principle of unrestrained official discretion has been given a fair trial, and it stands discredited by history. A mandatory disclosure system, limited in scope to information that the public urgently requires, would be administratively viable, consistent with the national security interest, and constitutionally superior.

We have no doubt that officials by and large would comply with routine disclosure requirements. Periodic reports submitted to Congress or published in the *Federal Register* are an established feature of the scene. Such requirements are always resented at first, but they tend to be rapidly assimilated into the bureaucratic routine.

The more nagging questions relate to the operation of our system in a crisis situation. In moments of grave danger, would our system deprive the nation of the ability to act with "vigor, secrecy and despatch?" We cheerfully concede that our proposals would deprive Presidents of the latitude to lead an unwitting nation into war; rigidity in this respect is essential. At the same time, our proposals are not intended to interfere with the successful prosecution of a constitutionally initiated war, and we cannot perceive any danger that they would do so. Outside the protected realm of specific military techniques, plans, and operations, situations demanding immediate, unilateral executive action should be few and far between.

We are persuaded that it would be a terrible mistake to provide for exceptions to the automatic disclosure requirements. We grant that a situation could conceivably someday arise in which compliance would be utterly disastrous. If the President made such a determination in a responsible manner, we are confident that the country would understand it. In a sense, every law contains an unwritten exception for such occasions. On the other hand, to provide expressly for exceptions would simply invite wholesale evasion of the disclosure requirements themselves. This has already occurred in the case of the "automatic" declassification procedures of the executive order, as well as the Church Amendment's provision for public reporting of executive agreements. It would be far better to shorten the list of disclosure categories than to eviscerate the entire system in this manner.

The proposal that Congress designate certain kinds of information as presumptively secret is scarcely novel. Congress has already legislated special protection for atomic energy information and cryptographic information. We propose to extend this approach to a few other areas in which secrecy is unlikely to prejudice the public interest.

Some controversy is possible respecting one of our categories, namely that of weapons design. As we noted above, respected scientists have argued that secrecy in this area actually inhibits the development of our own technology far more than it obstructs the research efforts of other nations. We do not feel equipped to evaluate this argument but expect that Congress would wish to do so very carefully.

As was true for our automatic disclosure categories, we anticipate that others may propose additions to our list of presumptive secrets. We are open to such suggestions and confident that Congress would have ample opportunity to consider them.

Whatever the list may ultimately contain, the logic of our analysis requires some provision for disclosure of information in the presumptively secret categories. No matter how narrowly the categories are drawn, instances are apt to arise where the case for disclosure is exceptionally compelling: for instance, in connection with debate over arms control proposals or with oversight of the intelligence community. If Congress enacts a flat rule of secrecy that could cover such situations, the executive branch will certainly not waive it under these circumstances.

We recognize that this position contrasts with our unwillingness to provide for similar exceptions to the automatic disclosure categories. The two situations are not analogous, because the incentive structure of the executive branch is not symmetrical. In the case of disclosure requirements, any exception would be sure to swallow the rule. No such danger is evident with respect to a rule of presumptive secrecy.

To justify the existence of a middle category should not require extended discussion. While we have argued at length against the system of unlimited official discretion, we do not believe that such discretion can or should be entirely eliminated. The legal designation of mandatory disclosure and presumptive secrecy categories is an appropriate way of dealing with a few specific kinds of information. Those are cases where the balance between the values of secrecy and disclosure can meaningfully be determined in advance, without reference to particular circumstances. However, the attempt to assign all national security information to one or the other of these categories would be extremely unrealistic and counterproductive. In most cases, a rational decision will require a sensitive weighing of the requirements of national security and of public debate in the particular situation. The initial decision must be left to responsible officials of the executive branch. Yet careful provision for the guidance of those officials is obviously essential.

In the past, the executive branch has not been accustomed to taking responsibility for the interest in public debate. That interest has not been central to the political environment in which the national security bureaucracy operates; nor has it been emphasized by the formal rules that apply to secrecy decisions. The executive order on classification does not instruct officials to balance the need for publicity against the need for secrecy; rather, their task is simply to determine whether secrecy would serve the broadly defined national security interest. In practice, it appears that public debate has been regarded as inherently prejudicial to the national security, and that documents have consciously been classified, under color of law, for the express purpose of preventing public debate.

It was not so long after Watergate that a staff official of the National Security Council made this reply to a request under the Freedom of Information Act:

> In addition, knowledge that the United States had undertaken a study of a particular issue could arouse the interest of special-interest groups in the United States which could mount a lobbying effort in the Congress and elsewhere in an effort to influence the outcome of the study and the decision or its recommendations. This could interfere seriously with the objective, dispassionate atmosphere in which these issues are analyzed and presented to the President and could have an inhibiting effect on the candor and completeness of the information and advice essential to the President in carrying out his responsibilities and, indeed, on the President's flexibility in dealing with the issue.[16]

Our proposals would reverse the presumption that public debate is a dangerous and inappropriate process. Instead we would establish a rule that information should be made public unless a convincing case can be made for withholding it from foreign governments. Officials who favor disclosure for reasons of their own will then have stronger legal support than they do today. Yet these formal changes will not by themselves reverse the preponderant incentives for secrecy inside the executive branch. It would be unrealistic to expect that adoption of new criteria will automatically lead to dramatic changes in official attitudes.

To encourage a responsible exercise of the official discretion applicable to the middle category of information, we propose a simpler, more transparent set of classification procedures, including a provision for outside review of agency decisions.

New Procedures for Classification

The classification process would begin with a careful review of any new document by the responsible official, who would first identify any information bearing on national security. Then he or she would determine whether the information fell into a specific statutory category for automatic release or presumptive secrecy. If not, the information would be marked for release, unless the official concluded that release could result in costs to national security that, even discounted by their improbability, clearly outweigh the value of the information for public debate.[17]

This three-step decision might be reflected in a corresponding three-part designator for each item of national security information. The second subhead would identify the relevant statutory category, if any; the third would indicate the appropriate disposition. Typical examples might be:

National Security Information/Combat Activity/Release;
National Security Information/Weapons Design/Withhold;
National Security Information/None/Release.

For the purpose of determining whether information is to be made public, only this system of designation would be used. The President would be permitted to establish or maintain additional designations to control distribution and storage of information that is properly withheld from the public under the above criteria. The names and meanings of all special designators, however, would be made public.

New legislation should reinforce the Nixon executive order's attempt to limit the agencies and the number of individuals who can classify information. It should require a classifier personally to sign the order that classifies the information, and to specify clearly which specific pieces of information in each document fit which categories. Where a document has merely copied a sentence or piece of information that had previously been classsified, the new document must specify the original document, identify the original classifier as well as the derivative classifier, and indicate clearly which information is derivatively classified.

Finally, our proposal would provide for the routine release of all information three years after classification, unless the head of the agency concerned specifically determines that the information merits reclassification. The decision in that event, however, would be left to an independent classification review board.

A Classification Review Board

Congress should create an independent Classification Review Board to assist it in overseeing the administration of a legislated classification system. The agency might be headed by a board of seven members, nominated by the President and subject to Senate confirmation. They should be appointed for extended, staggered terms. A number of different functions would be assigned to this board, which would have unqualified access, by subpoena if necessary, to all national security information.

The board would be notified automatically of all classification decisions and would be responsible for maintaining an unclassified index of all withheld information. Provisions for such an index are found in the implementing directives under the current executive order, but the task has not been done. Since the criteria and procedures outlined here would lead to a substantial reduction in the amount of information withheld, indexing would become substantially easier to carry out.

The Classification Review Board would be responsible for the release of information more than three years old, though the head of the classifying agency would be able to apply to the Review Board for extension of the period of secrecy. Admittedly, if confronted with a high-level certification that certain information must be kept secret in the interest of national defense or foreign policy, the Review Board would be likely to concur. Still, the procedure provides some further protection against bureaucratic abuse.

The Board should also be empowered to seek release of information less than three years old. Whether acting on its own initiative, on the request of a member of Congress, or on the appeal of a citizen pursuant to the Freedom of Information Act, the Board would first request reclassification by the classifying agency and would then make its own review of the agency's disposition. In cases under the Freedom of Information Act, the Board's decision would of course be subject to judicial review. Congress might wish to provide for judicial review of Board decisions in other instances as well.

Another function of the classification board would involve the deletion of properly classified information from certain current documents, particularly studies produced by the intelligence community, and their public release. The Central Intelligence Agency, the Bureau of Intelligence and Research in the State Department, and, to a lesser extent, the intelligence agencies in the Department of Defense produce many analyses of the world events that would be of great value to Congress and the public. These documents are often classified merely because they contain a relatively small amount of information obtained from clandestine sources. In many cases, an unclassified version of these documents could be produced with a very small amount of effort. At the present time, there is is no staff with either the responsiblity or the resources to perform this function. The Classification Board, in cooperation with the intelligence community, could render a valuable service in this connection.

The Interagency Classification Review Committeee established by President Nixon's executive order has had little impact, because it functions in a largely passive manner and without high visibility. Moreover, its caseload has been modest and its attitude relatively accepting of the bureaucratic fetish for secrecy. We expect that a more independent agency with more initiative and responsibility would have substantially greater effect.

The Role of the Courts

Our proposals would be incomplete if we did not address the question of their relationship to the Freedom of Information Act, the espionage laws, and the case law of prior restraint. These laws intersect with the present classification system to a very limited extent;[18] here we focus on the role that Congress should assign to the Courts in enforcing our proposed system.

In addition to the independent review board, a most effective mechanism to ensure that our proposed guidelines are followed would be one encouraging the press and the public to take the initiative in requesting particular information and forcing a timely review of the need for secrecy, first by the classifying agency and ultimately by the courts. This mechanism is of course already established in the Freedom of Information Act. However, a number of changes in legislation would flow naturally from adoption of the sort of classification system that we proposed. First the FOIA would have to be amended so that the (b)(1) exemption referred to classification criteria established by *legislation* rather than by executive order.[19] Legislation would also be needed to clarify the role of the proposed Classification Review Board in processing FOIA requests. One possibility would provide for an appeal to the Review Board prior to judicial review, where the agency refuses to release a requested document. A more expeditious approach would involve the Board directly in judicial proceedings. The courts might wish to call upon the Board from time to time for various sorts of assistance, such as the location of documents or the provision of expert testimony. However, it would be counterproductive to compromise the Board's independence by placing it in the position of representing the interests of the executive branch in litigation. Even more unfortunate would be the erosion of judicial independence that might result from excessive reliance on the advice of the Review Board. Thus any provision for Review Board participation in judicial proceedings must be drafted with great care.

The most far-reaching consequence of the new classification system for FOIA litigation would flow directly from enactment of the new classification criteria themselves. The court's first task would now be to determine whether the requested information fell into a required disclosure category. If it did, the inquiry would end there. Otherwise, the court would balance the respective public interests in secrecy and disclosure—rather than simply evaluating, as under the present system, the degree of harm that might flow from disclosure.

We would argue that his new balancing task, far from presenting insuperable difficulties, will often be a more congenial task for the courts than is the judgment required by the current system. The balancing of asserted governmental interests (e.g., law and order) against the imperatives of free and full debate is familiar to the courts in the context of First Amendment cases. Often these cases can be disposed of without the need for close analysis of the governmental interest involved, simply on the strength of the competing First Amendment interest. In FOIA cases, similarly, the court would often be able to find that the interest in disclosure is entitled to prevail, even if the harms asserted by the government would in fact come about.

We recognize that cases of some sensitivity will arise from time to time; but in the context of clear legislated guidelines the courts will be conceptually and politically well-equipped to proceed. Indeed, we think the judicial function has been far more unkindly used by executive attempts to enforce secrecy by *ex parte* proceedings, secret evidence, and other departures from traditional notions of due process.[20]

Prior Restraints

As the Supreme Court emphasized in the Pentagon Papers case, proposals for prior restraint come before the courts bearing an especially heavy presumption against their constitutionality. While the threat of subsequent punishment may inhibit free expression, prior restraint prevents it outright. When the first Congress approved the Bill of Rights, they may or may not have intended to bar prosecutions for seditious libel, but the First Amendment's injunction against abridging freedom of the press was, above all, meant to rule out schemes for prior censorship. Indeed, we think a persuasive case has been made for the proposition that all prior restraints on publication are unconstitutional.[21]

Be that as it may, the nation survived for nearly two hunded years without resorting to formal prior restraints on political speech. Even in wartime, voluntary press self-censorship was found sufficient to protect the national security. In the Internal Security Act of 1950, the high point of Cold War antisubversive legislation, Congress stated flatly that nothing in the act should be read as authorizing prior restraints. Only in the Atomic Energy Act did Congress make provision for court injunctions against disclosure. That very narrow provision has never been invoked, and its constitutionality remains to be tested in court.

Despite the absence of legislative backing for prior restraints, the executive branch has recently made two bold attempts to enjoin publication of national security information.

In the *Pentagon Papers* case the Supreme Court, while denying the requested injunction, intimated that such an order would be appropriate if the government could prove that publication would inevitably cause direct, immediate, and irreparable harm to the national security.[22] If Congress adopts a new classification system, including presumptive secrecy for specific kinds of information, the executive branch may well assert that all such information has been determined by Congress to meet the Supreme Court's standard for prior restraints. However, the argument for presumptive secrecy is not that disclosure would necessarily be disastrous; it is simply that the information is of little value to the American public and of some value to foreign governments. We believe that very little of this information in fact meets the Supreme Court's rigorous test. To remove all doubt, a new classification act should expressly disclaim any intent to authorize prior restraints.

In the *Marchetti* case, the Court of Appeals has upheld a permanent injunction, requiring Marchetti to submit all his writings to the CIA so that classified information can be deleted.[23] The court justified this wholly unprecedented order by invoking secrecy agreements Marchetti signed during his tenure as a CIA official. Congress has not authorized such agreements, much less the sweeping waiver of First Amendment rights they are now said to entail. Before the *Marchetti* decision, the congressional hands-off attitude toward prior restraints seemed satisfactory. We think

Congress must now act to limit the impact of secrecy agreements, exercising its power to regulate the terms of government employment.

The guidelines we would recommend flow naturally from the approach that has informed this entire study. Because of the special constitutional status of prior restraints, the degree of threatened harm must of course be exceedingly high before such action can be justified. Mr. Justice Stewart's standard of "inevitable, direct, immediate and irreparable harm" is strict enough as far as it goes. We submit, in addition, that the courts should be required to balance the expected harm, however great, against the value of the information to the American public. For, in the long run, secrecy is capable of causing harms every bit as grave as those it is meant to avert.

A final point relates to the question of temporary restraints during litigation. In the *Pentagon Papers* case, the delay in publication caused by issuing a temporary restraining order was of little practical moment. In other cases, such a delay might permit the government to accomplish its entire purpose even though the courts ultimately refused to issue an injunction. Where the timing of disclosure is critical, we think that even temporary restraints should not be approved until the government has made a very substantial showing of need and the defendant has been afforded the opportunity to rebut that showing.

Legal Sanctions

We have criticized the existing system for its informality and boundless flexibility, and in its place we have proposed the legislation of clear, authoritative guidelines as a feasible and effective avenue to reform. Some readers may feel that this line of thought points naturally, indeed inevitably, to the enactment of tough penalties designed to deter all unauthorized disclosures and all improper secrecy under the new guidelines. The idea is not without superficial appeal; but further reflection has persuaded us that to rely excessively on formal sanctions would be a serious mistake. In considering this matter we have been guided above all by an acute awareness of the practical limitations on what can be achieved by formal sanctions.

First of all, most officials, we believe, will obey the law when it is clearly and authoritatively expressed; they will do so not from fear of punishment but because their sense of professional integrity demands it. The post-Watergate climate is especially supportive of such a conscientious attitude.

In contrast, it is clear that even the strictest sanctions will not entirely put an end to leaks or to improper secrecy. Organizational communication patterns in the real world never conform to the simplicity of a formal code, and departures from the rule are inevitable when it comes to behavior that is both highly motivated and difficult to detect.

These general considerations indicate that formal sanctions should not be essential to achieve substantial compliance with our new guidelines; and that substantial compliance is as much as we can expect even if tough sanctions are enacted. By far the most compelling argument against tough legal sanctions, however, is the probability that they would backfire. Enforcement of administrative or criminal sanctions will necessarily be the responsibility, in the first instance, of the executive branch; and the performance of this function is necessarily a matter of discretion. Congress may enact balanced guidelines with symmetrical sanctions, but enforcement cannot be expected to be evenhanded.

As far as Presidents and their immediate subordinates are concerned, neither administrative nor penal sanctions will be a credible deterrent. For these officials it is obvious that the important sanctions must continue to come from outside the executive branch. Our proposed reforms will substantially assist Congress and the public in pressing for openness and responsibility at the highest levels by resolving doubts about the applicable norms and by legitimizing the conduct of officials who learn of improprieties and would wish to make them known to Congress or to the public. The ultimate impact of our proposals will depend, as it must, on the degree and tenacity of congressional and public concern about the issues.

Junior officials are less amenable to external, political controls; no doubt they would be more responsive to threatened administrative or criminal sanctions for violations of a classification law. Yet in view of the value structure that prevails within the executive branch, one would expect formal sanctions to be applied far more zealously for leaking than for improper withholding of information. Thus in recent years, officials who lied to Congress and the public about Cambodia and other matters have continued to receive promotions and new appointments, while whistleblowers continue to risk ostracism, loss of employment, or worse. The net result of tougher sanctions could easily be a further entrenchment of secrecy, instead of the hoped-for change to a more open and balanced system. In short, we believe that to emphasize a system of formal sanctions, even if it is well-balanced on paper, would only serve to strengthen the prevailing incentives for promiscuous secrecy.

This does not mean that the classification system we propose ought to be altogether toothless. In particular, career officials in whom the authority to classify is vested should be subject to periodic evaluation of their performance under the law. To facilitate such review, officials might be required to keep a logbook of their classification decisions, showing by category the number of items they have ordered released and withheld.

The Freedom of Information Act already provides for investigation by the Civil Service Commission in cases where a court finds that information may have been arbitrarily and capriciously withheld. Freedom of information audits on a routine basis could bring to light a larger number and a broader range of abuses; and the withdrawal of classification authority from severe or habitual violators of the statutory guidelines and procedures would be an appropriate sanction.

Even more valuable would be a stipulation that no sanctions be imposed on officials who release information that has been improperly withheld from the public.

Criminal Penalties

The secrecy system has never depended to any significant degree on the threat of criminal penalties. The Federalists' short-lived experiment in 1798-1800 with criminal libel trials did not encourage later administrations to do likewise. Until 1911 the United States had no espionage laws at all. The present statutes, which in essence date from 1917, were directed primarily at outright spying. Despite some legal ambiguity, officials of the Justice Department and legal advisers of national security agencies did not believe that leaking—much less the publishing of leaked information—was a crime unless there was a specific intent to injure the national defense. Before 1972 espionage indictments were brought only when it could be charged that information was passed directly to foreign agents. While officials receiving clearances were routinely warned that unauthorized disclosures could entail unspecified criminal penalties, these admonitions lacked visibility and credibility. They had little effect on the conduct of career officials and even less on that of political appointees.

The indictment of Daniel Ellsberg and Anthony Russo in connection with the disclosure of the Pentagon Papers marked the first effort to use the espionage laws to punish unauthorized publication. Although that indictment bore the taint of Watergate and did not result in a conviction, Justice Department officials continue to assert that it rested on a sound legal basis. The threat of indictment has become a factor to reckon with for officials and former officials who would release secret information to the press. Moreover, one of the same laws could, on its face, be invoked directly against private citizens who receive or publish classified information.

In the context of the present classification system, the claim that all classified information is protected by criminal sanctions is simply intolerable. The threat of prosecution, if taken seriously, would have a broad, chilling effect on public debate, which cannot be justified by the goal of preventing serious harm to national security. To remove the ambiguities that make this threat possible, Congress should repeal the laws under which Ellsberg and Russo were indicted.[24]

We think there are overwhelming legal and political objections to the use of criminal penalties against private citizens who receive or publish national security information. While objections to criminal penalties against *officials* for disclosing classified information would not be quite so overwhelming if Congress adopted the new classification system we propose, we have serious reservations both as to the need for such penalties and as to their impact. The nation survived two World Wars and the Cold War without sweeping restrictions on public debate; we see no need in this period of détente for a new "Official Secrets Act."

Certainly there should not be criminal penalties for any and all official disclosures of classified information. Even under a vastly improved classification system, there will be many difficult decisions and many opportunities for official error. The threat of prosecution for misclassification or for leaking will not encourage careful and objective judgments but will instead perpetuate the timid, self-protective attitude that now prevails. Frequent prosecutions would surely have a dulling effect both on public debate and on bureaucratic efficiency; while occasional and selective enforcement would undermine the credibility of deterrence and invite charges of politically motivated discrimination.

A better case can be made for criminal sanctions limited to the release of information designated by law as presumptively classified. Atomic energy and cryptographic information, in particular, are relatively narrow and well-defined categories. We think this highly technical information can be strictly protected without serious danger of interference with public debate. Criminal laws for this purpose already exist; they have rarely been invoked,[25] and we see no urgent need to change them. Nevertheless, we would not recommend extending this approach to our other categories of presumptively classified information. Cases will inevitably arise where information that arguably falls into a presumptively classified category is essential for legitimate public debate. The social cost of deterring disclosure in such cases outweighs the limited contribution to national security that criminal penalties would make.

Behind these concerns lies the overriding imperative of

evenhandedness. If there are to be criminal sanctions for disclosure of presumptively classified information, there must be criminal penalties as well for withholding information that Congress has designated for release. Surely the threat of prosecution is a crude and ineffective technique for compelling disclosure of such information. Officials will not expect the Justice Department to prosecute unless public opinion is very much aroused. Yet if Congress and the public are vigorous in demanding release of needed information and condemning those who resist, it will not be necessary to resort to criminal penalties.

In short, we believe that administrative and political sanctions are a more credible and appropriate approach than criminal penalties to the problem of evenhanded enforcement of a new classification system. Criminal penalties may safely be reserved for cases of outright spying, as they have been ever since Jefferson's day. It cannot be overstressed that the most effective protection for legitimate secrets would come from a rebirth of respect for the classification system, brought about by a stripping away of unnecessary secrecy. As Mr. Justice Stewart put it in the *Pentagon Papers* case:

> When everything is classified, then nothing is classified, and the system becomes one to be disregarded by the cynical or the careless, and to be manipulated by those intent on self-protection or self-promotion. I should suppose, in short, that the hallmark of a truly effective internal security system would be the maximum possible disclosure, recognizing that secrecy can best be preserved only when credibility is truly maintained.[26]

Chapter 6

The Constitutional Argument

he modern growth of presidential power has prompted corresponding innovations in constitutional doctrine. Recent Presidents have sponsored a remarkable development in the theory of implied or "inherent" presidential powers—powers that are not expressly granted by the Constitution, but are said to be justified by necessity. Originally, such powers were resorted to in emergencies that arose when Congress was not in session, with the understanding that congressional approval would be soqght as soon as possible. Recently, however, it has become fashionable to claim that the exercise of inherent presidential powers is immune to congressional or judicial interference. The executive branch is likely to insist, therefore, that the Constitution prohibits Congress from legislating a classification system that includes mandatory disclosure requirements; and that it prohibits the courts, with or without congressional approval, from reviewing executive secrecy decisions.

Certainly the Constitution itself does not support these assertions.

Several provisions of the Constitution bear directly on governmental powers to withhold information or duties to supply it. Two clauses are the heart of the constitutional plan for formal communication from the legislature to the people. The Framers saw the public's political role in terms of two key functions: voting for congressmen and paying taxes. It was essential, therefore, to inform the people as to how their representatives had voted and how their taxes were spent. Thus, Article I, section 5, provides that both Houses of Congress shall publish journals of their proceedings, "except such parts thereof as may in their judgment require secrecy." The history of this provision is quite complex, but the records of the Constitutional Convention and ratification debates show clearly that the Framers wished to provide for secrecy in such matters as wartime military operations and delicate diplomatic negotiations. When objections were raised to the latitude of the quoted clause, it was insisted by all that secrecy would be limited to the most compelling situations only: in John Marshall's words, to cases when it would be "fatal and pernicious to publish the schemes of government."[1]

For Article I, section 9, which requires that Congress periodically publish an account of public expenditures, there is little explanatory material available. The Framers, however, made no provision for secrecy in the spending of public funds.

Nor is there a constitutional provision for direct communication between the President and the people; remember, the President was not popularly elected at first. Instead, Article II, section 3, requires the President periodically to inform Congress of the State of the Union, and to recommend such measures as he shall judge necessary and expedient.

In marked contrast to the provision in Article I for congressional secrecy, the Framers gave the President no privilege to withhold information from Congress. The value they placed on secrecy in national security affairs was adequately protected, in their view, by the way the relevant decision-making functions were allocated.

They enumerated these presidential powers respecting national security:

The President shall be Commander in Chief of the Army and Navy of the United States, and of the militia of the several

States, when called into the actual service of the United States.

He shall have power, by and with the Advice and Consent of the Senate, to make treaties, provided two-thirds of the Senators present concur; and he shall nominate, and by and with the advice and consent of the Senate, shall appoint ambassadors . . . .

. . . he shall receive ambassadors and other public ministers.[2]

Congress, meanwhile, was expressly granted the following powers:

To declare war, grant letters of marque and reprisal, and make rules concerning captures on land and water;

To raise and support armies, but no appropriation of money to that use shall be for a longer term than two years;

To provide and maintain a navy;

To make rules for the government and regulation of the land and naval forces;

To provide for calling forth the militia to execute the laws of the Union, suppress insurrections and repel invasions;

To provide for organizing, arming, and disciplining the militia, and for governing such part of them as may be employed in the service of the United States, reserving to the States respectively, the appointment of the officers, and the authority of training the militia according to the discipline prescribed by Congress.[3]

The Framers had devoted much thought to the structuring of these national security powers. It was their aim to provide a foundation for more energetic leadership than the nation had enjoyed under the Articles of Confederation, while at the same time guarding against the sort of tyranny that had inspired the rebellion against the Crown. The Convention's debates abound with references to this tension between "vigor, secrecy, and despatch" on the one hand and "responsibility" on the other.[4] Where the allocation of the treaty-making power was concerned, the Framers settled upon a characteristic compromise: in the interest of protecting diplomatic secrecy, the House of Representatives (a large and "popular" body) was given no treaty role, but the Senate's participation as a sort of executive council was deemed essential to prevent the President from controlling the conduct of foreign affairs in the interest of his state or region.[5] Thus, it emerged that the most sensitive national security matters were confided to the care of the President and Senate, who were expected to work intimately together. Secrecy was considered appropriate and practicable for this small, select decision-making group. The role of the House was to be secondary, in part because of the difficulty of keeping secrets in so large a body. Nevertheless, the House was empowered to participate in decisions to declare war, to raise and support armies, and to regulate foreign commerce. These functions obviously would require some access to sensitive information, and therefore the House, too, was given power to withhold that information from the public.

These arrangements made sense as far as they went, being fully consistent with the seemingly obvious principle that each official or private citizen is entitled to all the information required to exercise his constitutional privileges and duties. Yet, the sharing of concurrent powers is inherently pregnant with controversy; and, for better or for worse, no formal mechanism was provided for resolving disputes about the precise application of this principle.

Whatever the Framers' actual expectations may have been, they failed to specify an explicit role for the courts in resolving constitutional disputes. In the controversies of the early years over the respective powers of Congress and the presidency with regard to secrecy and publicity, the possibility of judicial arbitration was not discussed.[6]

For all practical purposes, the function of judicial review did not yet exist. By the time the process became available, the problem of congressional access to national security information had lost political urgency. Many years were to pass before important secrecy-related issues were bought before the courts. In fact, only in the last few years has the political basis for major judicial involvement in this area fully matured.[7]

Thus, most of the "precedents" on the right to gain or withhold information consist not of authoritative legal principles, but of self-serving, often extreme, claims advanced by executive and congressional spokesmen over the years. These claims have typically been tailored to the political needs of the moment and have not been strictly consistent over time; moreover, no clear and firm consensus has ever developed between the executive and legislative branches concerning their respective powers. In general, the matter has been left on a political, rather than a legal footing.[8]

This sporadic, informal control system has been disastrously ineffective in recent years; as we have argued, the problem today is structural rather than transitory. It would be fallacious to assume that a history of nonregulation creates a legal bar to needed regulatory action. In fact, there is no constitutional obstacle to our proposals. This is abundantly clear from a review of the relevant decisions of the Supreme Court.

Inherent Presidential Powers and the Role of Congress

The Court has decided very few cases relating to the allocation of national security powers among the branches of government and even fewer relating to control of information. Such questions are seldom directly presented in litigation between private parties or between a private party and the government as a whole. In these contexts, executive acts are usually claimed to have been authorized or ratified by Congress, and the Court has preferred not to scrutinize too closely this image of cooperative decision-making. Thus the Court has held that congressional approval may properly be given in very general terms, may be implicit rather than direct, and may take place after the fact. These decisions have legitimized the historical accretion of national security powers to the Presidency—a development the Court surely has not been in a position to contain.

Since the Civil War the Commander-in-Chief clause has emerged as an important source of presidential power, and it is now conceded that he may, even without specific congressional authority, employ military force, at least when U.S. territory or forces are under attack; create executive offices necessary to prosecute a war; issue regulations affecting industry and labor in wartime; requisition property in a theater of war; establish procedures for military government in occupied territory; and end hostilities by armistice.[9]

At the same time, the Senate's failure to establish an active role in diplomacy has left the President as the sole organ for contacts with foreign governments. In this capacity he can grant recognition to foreign governments, negotiate, interpret, and terminate treaties, negotiate executive agreements, and appoint personal agents, (including secret agents) to gather information.[10]

The rationale for these implied powers has been that unity and rapid decision are necessary for the effective conduct of war and diplomacy. While the Court and the nation have agreed that Presidents need not wait for congressional action before taking emergency measures, it does not follow, and the Court has never held, that emergency justifies action that is flagrantly illegal, or that is kept secret once the immediate crisis is past.

Indeed, the Court has repeatedly made it clear that the President's emergency powers are limited by the concurrent powers of the other branches and by the Bill of Rights. In the last analysis it remains the province of Congress to make the law and that of the Court to ensure that the fundamental constitutional rights of citizens are respected.[11]

The claim that Congress may not legislate limits on presidential national security powers is not supported by precedent. A careful review of Supreme Court decisions shows that only the pardon power and the power to fire presidential appointees have been accorded a measure of immunity from legislative interference.[12]

The Court has never held any congressional act to be unconstitutional on the ground that it infringed the President's powers as Commander-in-Chief or as agent of foreign policy. Instead, the Court has uniformly held that once Congress addresses itself to a particular national security problem, the President is bound by the legislation and is not free to pursue alternative measures that are more to his liking.[13]

The cases most often cited in support of Presidential claims to "inherent" or exclusive national security powers[14] do show that the President may take substantial initiatives on his own where Congress has established no specific restrictions; and that the President and Congress, acting together, have ample powers—always limited by the Bill of Rights—to do what the national security requires. These cases do not discuss, and certainly in no way limit the power of Congress to establish guidelines and procedures for the conduct of the executive branch.

Presidents themselves have recognized the propriety and usefulness of congressional participation in the secrecy system. They have sought and obtained special legislation protecting atomic energy, intelligence and cyptographic secrets, and more recently have proposed additional legislation protecting classified information in general. If Congress may legislate for secrecy, surely it may legislate for publicity as well.

The Role of the Courts

In vetoing the 1974 amendments to the Freedom of Information Act, President Ford asserted that the provision for *de novo* judicial review of security classifications is unconstitutional. This assertion was not backed by supporting argument, and Congress did not find it persuasive. Nevertheless, a summary of the applicable case law is helpful in showing how little authority can be mustered for the President's view.

It is true that the courts have no explicit constitutional role in making national security policy. That function is assigned to the popularly elected, "political" branches of government. This legal separation is reinforced by the courts' desire to avoid potentially damaging accusations of irresponsible meddling in national security affairs—not to mention charges of deliberate subversion.

Thus, they have been most reluctant to judge matters of national security policy, to become involved in disputes between Congress and the President, or even to review factual determinations by Congress or the President that relate to national security. Corwin has summarized the scope of this principle as follows:

On this principle the Court has subsequently held at one time or
another that it must accept as final and binding on itself the
determinations of one or other or both of "the political
departments," with respect to all such questions as whether a
certain newly constituted community was a qualified belligerent
at international law; what was the correct boundary of a certain
country; what country was the sovereign of a particular region;
whether a certain community was entitled to be considered as a
"belligerent" or as an independent state; who was the *de jure*,
who the *de facto* ruler of a certain country; whether a particular
person was a duly accredited diplomatic agent to the United
States; how long a military occupation of a certain region
should continue in order to fulfill the terms of a treaty; whether
a certain treaty was in effect; and so on.[15]

This commitment to self-restraint, however, has never entailed
an abdication of what the courts see as their essential functions.
They have always reserved the power to balance governmental
interests, however urgent, against the fundamental rights of citizens,
and steadfastly refused to relinquish control over the conduct of
judicial proceedings. The judicial temper is well illustrated by a
recent case in which the government argued that the supervision of
national security wiretaps was beyond judicial competence. To this
attack on Fourth Amendment rights the court responded vigorously:

> If the threat is too subtle or complex for our senior law
> enforcement officers to convey its significance to a court, one
> may question whether there is probable cause for surveillance.[16]

In one line of cases the courts have considered the extent of
their own power, in the absence of statutory guidelines, to compel
the executive branch to supply evidence needed in court
proceedings.[17]

This issue has been treated in a gingerly fashion, whether the
executive resistance to disclosure was based on national security
concerns, or simply on a generalized policy of confidentiality for
high-level executive deliberations. Despite the courts' respectful
language and careful avoidance of confrontation whenever possible,

they have maintained the position that executive claims of privilege are not automatically binding. It is up to them to balance the need for secrecy against the litigating parties' need for information.

In four cases the Supreme Court drew back from ordering disclosure of national security information; these were the *Totten*, *Waterman, Reynolds,* and *Mink* cases cited above. *Totten* involved Union spying activities during the Civil War. *Waterman,* decided in 1948, had to do with the licensing of foreign operations for U.S. air carriers. *Reynolds* was about the crash of an airplane carrying secret electronic equipment; while *Mink* involved nuclear weapons testing.

In none of these cases did the court recognize a constitutional limitation on its power to demand information. In *Reynolds*, the privilege to withhold "state secrets" was expressly stated to rest on judicial discretion. The secrecy involved in *Totten* was at least indirectly authorized by law, in that Congress had long exempted the President's secret service expenditures from the usual budgetary disclosure requirements. Congress has also been especially solicitous to protect the kinds of information involved in *Waterman*, *Reynolds*, and *Mink*.

In fact, the Court said explicitly in both *Waterman* and *Mink* that its decision was simply an interpretation of legislative intent. In the former, it held that Congress did not intend to authorize judicial review and that this policy was constitutionally permissible. It was clearly implied that Congress could also have made the opposite choice without running afoul of any constitutional limitation. In *Mink*, the issue was the intent of Congress in passing the 1967 Freedom of Information Act. While holding that judicial review of security classifications had not been contemplated, the Court expressly invited Congress to legislate new disclosure guidelines if it saw fit. The Court certainly did not suggest that a provision for judicial review would be unconstitutional.[18]

It is easy to appreciate the value of a clear congressional mandate and legislated guidelines to assist the delicate function of judicial review of national security matters. The implementation of legislated guidelines is a far more congenial task, both politically and intellectually, than the independent development of judicial standards for balancing secrecy and disclosure values.

Nothing in the case law, therefore, even remotely suggests that the Freedom of Information Act is unconstitutional or that our proposals for further amendment would make it so. When officials oppose reforms that will disrupt established routine, they invariably argue that the government will be paralyzed by the plan. This bureaucratic shibboleth has not yet been elevated by the Court to the status of a constitutional principle.

Indeed, President Ford did not attempt to argue that the courts can play no role whatever in the secrecy system. The executive branch wishes to retain the option of seeking judicial aid in enforcing secrecy, but if the courts are competent to judge the need for secrecy, surely they may judge the need for publicity as well. In fact, President Ford conceded that it would be proper for a court to review a classification decision in order to decide whether it was reasonable. If so, we do not see how the Constitution can be said to prohibit the courts from going on to inquire whether a "reasonable" classification decision was, in fact, correct. That is all the new FOIA provision for *de novo* review accomplishes. While the formula preferred by the President might result in a somewhat smaller number of judicially ordered disclosures, it would not affect the basic quality of the proceedings. The evidence and the scope of the court's inquiry would be essentially the same; any difference could hardly rise to constitutional significance.

The Constitutional Case for a More Open System

We think it is perfectly clear that Congress, in order to rectify the balance between secrecy and publicity, can legislate a classification system and provide for judicial review of classification decisions. Nothing in the case law suggests otherwise.

Neither the text of the Constitution nor the interpretations evolved by the Supreme Court have designated the protection of national security as an exclusive function of the executive. Executive secrecy, moreover, poses a direct and serious threat to the essential functions of the other branches, and it cannot be supposed that the Constitution gives them no power to resist that threat. By the same token, safeguarding the democratic political process is not a function committed to the exclusive care of the executive branch. Publicity fosters the right to vote and to participate in political life; these concerns are well within the spheres of congressional and judicial competence.

While the Supreme Court has affirmed that presidential discretion in national security affairs is entitled to very great respect, it has also insisted that this discretion is limited by the powers of Congress, the rights of citizens, and the integrity of the judicial process. Nothing in the cases suggests, therefore, that Congress cannot legislate new guidelines for the withholding and release of national security information; nothing in them raises a constitutional obstacle to judicial enforcement, mandated by Congress, of such guidelines.

We would not be content, however, merely to argue that our proposals offend against no specific principle of constitutional law. In a somewhat broader sense the fundamental argument *in favor* of less secrecy about matters of foreign policy and national defense is constitutional. The Framers sought to design a structure for effective leadership that would not threaten liberty. Therefore Congress was charged with heavy, but not with everyday, responsibilities concerning foreign policy and national defense. Under the Constitution, it is Congress that must appropriate funds for the military and establish regulations for their operation. It is Congress that has the power of declaring war. Congress is responsible also for appropriating funds for the conduct of foreign relations, and has a special responsibility for the regulation of international commerce. The Senate, of course, has the power to approve treaties and confirm envoys. Congress can carry on none of these functions if it is in the dark about the activities of the executive branch. Nor can it exercise a wise discretion—however limited—if deprived of critical information available to the executive branch about the behavior of foreign governments.

While the executive branch insists that no information is ever denied to Congress simply because it is classified, this assertion is somewhat beside the point. For the way Congress uses the information it gets depends greatly on the status of the source. When classified information does come to the attention of Congress, it will be through secret briefings or through leaks. So long as the source cannot be identified and its official standing used to verify the information, the ability of a member of Congress or of Congress as a whole to use the information will be sharply impaired.

A member of Congress who is disturbed by secret information that he or she obtains is placed in a difficult position. Ordinarily, the support of colleagues for controversial measures is developed with the assistance of public speeches, public debate, and public exchanges with the executive branch. The nonpublic processes of informal consultation and bargaining among legislators work best when backed by the sanctions of public opinion. If there is no public demand for action, legislators have little incentive to take the tremendous risk of openly defying the executive branch by releasing the information and appealing for public support. Thus, members of Congress wishing to muster support for legislative countermeasures will often be unable to act until the supporting evidence can be made public. They are understandably tempted to leak the information, hoping to compel the executive branch to confirm or deny its accuracy and thus initiate a public debate. Yet this course, too, involves substantial risk and its propriety is always subject to doubt. Too often inaction is the result.

Examples of congressional frustration in using secret information are easy to find. In the House Judiciary Committee's impeachment investigation, the classified status of relevant information on the Cambodia bombing was apparently an obstacle to the committee's work. Their report contains the following footnote:

> Rep. Seiberling also stated that because of the President's decision not to declassify certain materials, such evidence could not be made public or be discussed during the Committee's debate. Rep. Seiberling said that this prevented the public use of certain documents which tied the President into acts of concealment. He stated that this was one of the reasons he opposed the Article.

The *non sequitur* quality of this member's reasoning does not nullify the conclusion that secret information is awkward for Congress to use. Senator George Aiken has described this problem as follows:

> We all know that when the appropriations bill is pending the Russians in particular become extremely powerful. They are on the verge of producing weapons which could virtually exterminate us at one blow and we have to do something about that right away. Let's assume (the Defense Department) asks for a trillion dollars to continue (its) research . . . .But assume that the members of the committee entitled to the information from the CIA learn that this information, so-called, which has been spread across the front pages of the press to justify the demand for a trillion dollars, isn't so; that the Russians are nowhere near that point in their development of destructive weapons and that say $500 billion would suffice to insure the security of the United States.
>
> What do we do then? Do we go on the floor and take the position against all this publicity which has been spread in public before the committees and spread before the United States and the press? Then to carry out our duties we vote against that trillion dollars . . . . and approve of only $500 billion. How do we justify that position with our constituents back home? Assuming we want to be reelected, it puts us in a bad spot. Can we say we got this information from the CIA? How do we justify our position after all this publicity has been made on the other side of it?
>
> You know self-preservation is a very strong instinct among Members of Congress.[19]

As we saw in Chapter 2, a few members of Congress had apparently received secret briefings about the bombing of Cambodia long before the story broke. A rumor had been leaked to the press as early as May 1969. Neither of these events produced any effective opposition, despite the changing complexion of public opinion and the grave constitutional significance of this exercise in presidential war-making. Nor was Senator Fulbright able to take any effective action when he received a copy of the Pentagon Papers through unauthorized channels.

As another example, the defense budget considered by Congress in late 1974 included a request for funds to complete a ballistic missile defense site. This was the only ABM installation that the United States was permitted to have under the revised Strategic Arms Limitation Treaty. Now Congress had been informed in secret that the Pentagon planned to dismantle the site as soon as it was completed. However, a vote against the ABM site would appear to the naive public to be directed against a serious military program. Because the plan to dismantle was secret, it was difficult for a member of Congress to vote against the appropriation. It was even difficult to bring this classified information to the attention of all members of Congress. Opponents of the appropriation were obliged to invite their colleagues individually to walk over to the desks of the managers of the bill, where they could read the classified statement. Few had the time or the interest to do so, and the appropriation was approved.[20]

Finally, several members of Congress knew of the recent intervention in Angola well before it became public. They felt they could only go along, despite serious misgivings, until public disclosure triggered a thorough examination of the objectives of the intervention and the prospect for success.

The clear lesson of these events is that Congress requires the informed support of public opinion in order to perform its constitutional role in the system of checks and balances. It is equally clear that citizens voting for their congressional representatives and their President need to understand what the major policies of incumbent officials have been and how well they have been carried out. Neither legislators nor the executive branch can effectively carry out policies in the long run that are not responsive to public opinion. The constitutional system does not run on blind faith, and the government cannot act resolutely without an adequate basis of public support. If the government needs to know what the people think of its policies, the people must know what those policies are.

We do not mean to equate the constitutional role of the public with that of Congress or to argue for government by referendum. The Framers certainly conceived of the public's role as a limited one. The Constitution did not give the people the power to instruct their representatives how to vote, nor does it expressly confer upon them a right to demand information from the government. Nevertheless, the First Amendment rights of petition, free speech, and freedom of the press can scarcely be meaningfully exercised if the public is kept ignorant of vital facts and policy decisions affecting the central obligations of citizenship and the central facts of life—taxes, military service, war and peace. In principle, the secrecy system is inimical to First Amendment values, and as such it bears a heavy burden of justification.

A further, serious constitutional indictment of the secrecy that now surrounds foreign policy and national defense matters arises from the effect that it has had and is likely to have on the civil liberties of Americans. When opponents of administration foreign policy resorted to leaks of closely held information, the Nixon administration undertook to deal with it by such unorthodox techniques as burglary and wiretapping, made unprecedented attempts at the prior restraint of publication, and brought the first "espionage" indictment against a person who was not claimed to be an agent of a foreign government. Although the national security rationale for these actions was neither factually nor legally convincing, the executive branch has never decisively repudiated these attacks on loyal citizens who challenged its claim to exclusive control of information and of the policy-making process.

Behind the pragmatic or theoretical arguments that are offered in support of this claim, there often lies an attitude of contempt for Congress and the public. Officials who are in possession of precious secrets unknown to the man in the street easily come to believe that they have the duty and privilege of lying to protect those secrets. Ultimately the protection of this privileged status begins to seem an end in itself; thus the "dirty tricks" routinely practiced in foreign affairs could come to be used also in a presidential reelection campaign.

Defenders of the secrecy system are fond of pointing to the existence of leaks in order to show that the problem of secrecy is not so serious as critics maintain. We have already shown why leaks cannot be relied upon to serve the purpose of informing Congress and the public. From a constitutional perspective, it should be clear that leaking is as much a part of the problem as of the solution. The prevalence of leaks, so often inspired by motives of bureaucratic, partisan, or diplomatic gamesmanship, reinforces the attitude that public opinion is a pawn in the game. Moreover, we have seen that leaking tends to provoke countermeasures that have serious implications for civil liberties.

The needs of Congress and the public for information, as well as the concern for civil liberties, argue that secrecy should be held to the unavoidable minimum in our constitutional system. The defenders of the status quo are not in a position to argue that this goal has been achieved. Numerous studies of the secrecy system have been sponsored by the executive branch and by Congress, including some whose primary purpose was to deal with the problem of leaks. Every such study has concluded that far too much information is kept secret, both in constitutional terms and in terms of sheer efficiency. No one seriously contends that the current level of secrecy is essential for an effective defense and foreign policy.[21]

The argument on which the executive branch relies is not that the current level of secrecy is in fact optimum, but that the necessary secrecy cannot be protected unless the present system of unilateral executive control is preserved and even strengthened. We think this argument goes too far toward equating the imperatives of national security with the institutional preeminence of the presidency and the unquestioning acceptance of administration policy. National security would not be better served by the triumph of this doctrine; on the contrary, the nation would benefit from a more open system.

Chapter 7

Some Concluding Remarks

The pressures for things to continue as they are remain very strong. The bureaucracy always fears the new because of its uncertain impact on power relations; but in the case of these proposals the thrust is not in doubt. As we have tried to demonstrate, control over information—the ability to release it or to keep it secret—is a major source of power within the bureaucracy. The experts in that maze will fight to keep that power; they will threaten dire consequences if the proposals presented here are implemented.

We will be told that the scheme is unworkable, a bureaucratic nightmare that will bring the business of government to a halt. We will be told that the scheme ignores the subtleties of the real world, that life is much more complicated than we make it out to be. In a world in which there are dangerous enemies out to destroy us, the executive branch must retain great flexibility to decide what information should be made public.

In Washington now the assumption remains that it is better to err on the side of secrecy, better not to release if some harm could ensue. The formal classification system and the Freedom of Information Act permit secrecy if there is a reasonable basis for believing that some harm to the national security will result, no

103

matter how important the information to public debate. Behind this now legitimate standard for secrecy, the system is used to prevent debate, to cover embarrassment, whether political or personal, and to manipulate the political process. That information would be used in public debate about major policies is not, from this perspective, a compelling and overriding argument for its release, but rather an argument for secrecy.

Nothing less than a radical change in perspective is implicit in the new system we propose. The presumptions must be turned around. Whatever is needed for public debate must be made public. The burden must be on those who would keep a secret. Foreign and defense policy must no longer be treated as the private preserve of the bureaucracy and the President. The decisions made in that arena affect the vital interests of all Americans and of many others throughout the world. Vast sums of public treasure are at stake, and, as we learned again in Vietnam, so may be many lives. If American democracy is to have meaning in its third century, public policy must emerge from the crucible of public debate and congressional as well as executive action.

This ideal is applicable to national security affairs as well as in other fields. Openness is not only constitutionally necessary but also consistent with American survival in a hostile world. Time and again we have seen arguments about the need for secrecy exposed for what they were: the overcautious predictions of those who simply prefer to work in secret—or covers to prevent the American public from learning the truth. The Pentagon Papers, which the Nixon White House went to court to keep secret, were published, and the Republic stood. If anything, it was strengthened by an understanding of how we were drawn into a national tragedy. The bombing of Cambodia was reported in the press yet it went on, despite the claim that secrecy was essential; and we know now that it was neither necessary nor sufficient to accomplish American objectives in Indochina, whatever those were or should have been. American intervention in Angola became public, necessitating executive requests for public funding to finance that campaign. What brought that escapade to an end was not irresponsible publicity but rather a congressional vote that it was not in the American interest to intervene.

The fact is that the security of the United States does not rest on the ability of the government to act in secret. Economically and militarily, we are an enormously powerful and secure nation. Our ability to repel attack does not depend on secrecy, except perhaps in those technical matters that we would permit to be kept secret. We would stand behind this proposal even if it involved some significant costs, but we emphasize that in our view that case has simply not been made.

We have no doubt that the majority of Americans would prefer less secrecy and are prepared to accept a modest risk to achieve it. The sorry consequences of excessive secrecy for our constitutional system, for our civil liberties, and for the promotion of our ideals and interests in the world are there for all to see.

We recognize that the adoption of a more open system might lead to substantive policy changes. Some of these might run counter to our own policy preferences. But broader participation is not only a constitutional value in itself; in the long run it is a political necessity. No policy that contemplates a sustained and substantial American commitment can sensibly be undertaken without a broad and informed base of support. Regardless of the policy's merits, disclosure could cause its abrupt collapse, as occurred in the case of Angola. A more open system, while responsive to changes in public opinion, would be protected against this kind of antisecrecy backlash.

The imperatives of our constitutional decision-making system and the practical need to evolve policies that have broad support are so great that we would favor a substantially more open system even if we believed that in the short run it would produce policies we do not support. In fact, we concede that adoption of a more open system might well interfere with certain aspects of national security policy as presently conceived. Admittedly, we hope that a more open system will result in significantly lower defense budgets and less intervention by the United States in the internal affairs of other countries. These changes, we are persuaded, would represent clear political gains without impairing the basic economic and military capabilities on which our security rests. And most certainly, national security cannot be endangered by a debate about the policies involved, or about the very process by which national policy is made and carried out. For instance, the nation has recently been engaged in reevaluating the proper role of the intelligence community and the mode of its accountability. The information about past operations that has leaked out has made it clear that secrecy has provided a cover for substantial abuses.[1] The claim that national security has suffered from these revelations is unsubstantiated and unpersuasive. If a more open system would prevent the recurrence or ensure the discovery of similar abuses in the future, that can only be counted as a gain.

Today, we have a new President committed to openness and without longstanding relationships to the bureaucratic secrecy system. The time is ripe for action. Yet, even so, the adoption of the type of system we propose will require strong initiative from Congress. That, in turn, requires pressure from the public. In this post-Vietnam/Watergate era it is perhaps not too much to hope that it will come. Our task, as we conceived it, was to provide a rationale and a blueprint. The ultimate test will be whether the American people still believe, with James Madison, that "A people who mean to be their own governors must arm themselves with the power which knowledge gives."[2] And whether we still have the will to govern ourselves.

Appendix A

The Espionage Laws

The espionage laws deal primarily with the offense of deliberate spying on behalf of foreign powers. In that context they have little impact on civil liberties or on the process of public debate. However, it is necessary to discuss them here because of the espionage indictments obtained by the Nixon administration in connection with the publication of the Pentagon Papers.

In the aftermath of the Ellsberg-Russo trial, it is clear that the espionage laws do stand in tension with First Amendment values. Although no conviction resulted from that trial, neither did it yield a definite ruling that would bar future indictments for publishing nontechnical but politically controversial information. Because this ambiguity may have a chilling effect on the process of public debate, reform of the espionage laws is an important objective in its own right.

The current espionage laws are in a state of total confusion. They form no coherent structure, and each part of them poses many complicated problems of interpretation. Neither the intended meaning nor even the literal meaning of the terms of each statute is obvious.[1]

This situation is not only intellectually awkward, but it raises constitutional questions as well. Not even the strict, absolutist devotees of the First Amendment have been able to discern a right to convey weapons secrets to a foreign power. We may take it that a ban on spying as such is clearly valid. But an espionage law may run afoul of the Constitution if it is overbroad, that is, if it also clearly covers speech protected by the First Amendment, or if it is so vague that one cannot tell what kind of behavior is made illegal, so that a chilling effect is cast on public debate.

The scope of a law affecting speech must be tailored to the danger that justifies the law. If it covers speech that is constitutionally protected as well as what is properly punished, the law is invalid.[2] The due process doctrine known as void-for-vagueness states the elementary notion that it is unfair to punish one who, with the best of will, could not have determined with any certainty whether or not his conduct would be a crime. Especially where the law impinges on freedom of speech, one is entitled to clear notice of what is prohibited.[3] Such notice certainly is not provided by the simple act of reading the espionage laws.

The Current Law

Until 1911 the United States had no espionage laws. It was in contemplation of American involvement in military conflict in Europe that a relatively simple law was passed in that year. Six years later, Congress passed the laws that are still, in virtually unchanged form, on the books today. In 1932 and in 1950, certain specialized laws were added, and in 1950 Congress made an important addition to the 1917 law. But the basic espionage laws are those passed in 1917.[4]

There appears to be a great gap between what Congress intended in passing the espionage laws in 1917 and what it actually wrote into the law. On the one hand, Congress vehemently rejected a scheme of publication controls proposed by President Woodrow Wilson, which, in its view, would have interfered with public debate. The 1917 law referred expressly to publication only in the context of wartime publication of military information "with intent that the same shall be communicated to the enemy." Thus Congress clearly disclaimed any general purpose to interfere with the publication of information, merely because it might eventually be used by a foreign power to its advantage or to the injury of the national defense. Yet other portions of the law do proscribe information-gathering and communication activities that might precede the publication of information related to the national defense, as well as its transmission directly to a foreign government. Moreover, portions of the law seem to apply to persons against whom the government can not allege any purpose of harming the national defense of the United States. In addition to the apparent gap between what Congress intended and what it actually enacted, in many cases the statutes defy any logical interpretation when examined closely and in relation to each other.

These ambiguities in the law have only recently been noticed. Until the Pentagon Papers episode in 1971, U.S. officials generally believed that the espionage laws (18 U.S.C. sections 793 and 794) applied only to genuine spies who sought to pass information to foreign agents with the intent, or at least reason to believe, that the information would be used by a foreign government to injure the United States or to aid that government.[5] Although this interpretation is not compelled by the language of the statutes, it was taken so seriously that the executive branch repreatedly declined to institute prosecution for leaks of classified information it regarded as serious. The government believed it could not indict, because there was not the requisite intent or reason to believe that the information would be used to injure the national defense.[6]

On several occasions Congress was asked by the executive branch for legislation to make criminal the release of any classified information by a present or former government official. These requests testify to the traditional belief inside the executive branch that leaking is not in general a violation of existing law.

It is true that officials given access to classified information were routinely warned that unauthorized disclosure could be a criminal act. But in practice, violations of the classification system were punished only by administrative action.

The congressional viewpoint was given in 1950, in the process of enacting a new criminal law protecting communications intelligence: "Under the Espionage Act of 1917, unauthorized revelation of information of this kind can be penalized only if it can be proven that the person making the revelation did so with an intent to injure the United States.[7]

This policy has been deliberate and consistent, and supported by self-interested as well as altruistic motives, for the extent of its own reliance on revelations by former officials has become quite apparent to Congress. There are frequent public hearings, as well as occasional ones in "executive" session, in which testimony is taken from those who have left government.[8] Their testimony has been of great importance to Congress, for example, in reviewing and developing alternatives on the defense budget. Moreover, congressional committees and individual congressmen and senators have recruited former officials for their staffs, intending to draw upon the knowledge and experience they have acquired. Much of that information would be considered "classified" in the executive branch or could be said to "relate to the national defense."

The congressional attitude toward more narrowly focused legislative proposals has been far more accepting. Congress has expressly made it a crime to publish classified information relating to atomic energy, communications intelligence, or codes. For example, in 1931 a former government official published a detailed account of American success in breaking Japanese diplomatic codes over the prior ten years. In 1933 it was learned that the same author was about to make further detailed revelations along these lines. Within a few weeks Congress passed legislation that made it a crime to publish cryptographic information, a quick response that prevented publication of the second book. According to the House report accompanying a more recent cryptographic bill, it was the intent of the House "while carefully avoiding the infringement of civil liberties" to provide protection covering "only a small category of classified matter, a category which is both vital and vulnerable to an almost unique degree." The narrow scope of this legislation can scarcely be viewed as inadvertent.[9]

In the aftermath of the Pentagon Papers episode, Congress

once again declined to act on an administration request for a broad Official Secrets Act. Hearings that were held at that time were not provoked by distress at the evil of leaking by former officials. Rather, the House Government Operations Committee and, later, three subcommittees of the Senate Judiciary and Government Operations committees held hearings on the evil of excessive classification of information. Congressional sentiment maintained that the executive branch ought itself to have released the Pentagon Papers prior to their publication in the *New York Times*. Bowing to pressure from these committees, the executive branch did agree to the publication of most of the material contained in the Pentagon Papers.[10]

We think this record makes an overwhelming case that Congress never intended the espionage laws to apply to leaks of nontechnical information.

The courts had no occasion prior to 1971 to express any opinion on that question. There have been, in fact, surprisingly few indictments even for actual spying. A few, involving alleged German espionage agents, occurred during World Wars I and II. After 1945 there were several indictments of alleged communist spies, the most notorious being those involving Julius and Ethel Rosenberg, Judith Coplon, and the Soviet spy Rudolf Abel. In all these cases, the government alleged that clandestine transfer of information to agents or officials of foreign governments had taken place. The legal disputes turned mainly on Fourth and Fifth Amendment questions involving search and seizure of evidence, wiretaps, or the illegality of confessions. The only higher court opinions that dealt with fundamental constitutional issues of relevance here were those in the cases of *Gorin, Heine,* and *Scarbeck.*

Gorin v. United States

The basic issue faced by the Supreme Court in *Gorin* was a challenge to the constitutionality of the law, directed specifically to the term, "relating to the national defense." Defendants argued that this term was fatally vague in meaning, unless construed as applying only to information about specific installations and objects mentioned elsewhere in the espionage laws: vessels, aircraft, forts, signal stations, and code books. The Court found no support in the legislative history for such a narrow construction and instead accepted the broad definition of national defense suggested by the government: national defense is a "generic concept of broad connotations, referring to the military and naval establishments and the related activities of national preparedness."[11]

The Court went on to say that although this phrase might appear on its face to be excessively vague, the statute was saved by its separate *scienter* (state of mind) requirement. That is, the government was obliged to prove that defendants acted "with intent or reason to believe" that the information they were obtaining was "to be used to the injury of the United States or to the advantage of any foreign power." If one were proved to have acted with such intent, the Court reasoned, he must have known that he was engaging in conduct that violated the statute. Therefore, the phrase "relating to the national defense" was not fatally vague.

This decision did not address the problem that would arise in applying other portions of the law to activities that clearly are not spying. In sections 793(d) and (e), there is no general requirement of "intent or reason to believe the information is to be used to injure the national defense"; here the mere transmitting to unauthorized persons of documents "relating to the national defense" is apparently made a crime. It is certainly arguable that in this unqualified context, the definition of "relating to the national defense" upheld in *Gorin* becomes so excessively vague and overbroad as to render the provisions unconstitutional.

United States v. Heine

In this Court of Appeals decision, authored by Judge Learned Hand, the main issue was whether collecting information from the public domain could be punished under the espionage statutes. As Judge Hand recognized, the term "relating to national defense" was to be broadly construed, and

. . .so drastic a repression of the free exchange of information it is wise carefully to scrutinize, lest extravagant and absurd consequences result.

It seems plain that the section cannot cover information about all those activities which become tributary to "the national defense" in time of war; for in modern war there are none which do not.[12]

The court found it possible, however, to avoid the impact of the holding in *Gorin* by addressing itself squarely to the question of criminal intent. From the *Gorin* decision, it was already clear that collection of information that the government had actually put into the public domain would not be punishable, because "where there is no occasion for secrecy . . . there can, of course, in all likelihood be no reasonable intent to give an advantage to a foreign government."[13] In *Heine*, the information had been gathered entirely from public sources and had never, in fact, been classified. Declining to distinguish information released by the government from that which was never secret, the Court concluded that the gathering of information entirely from public sources, as Heine had done, could not be a crime. Judge Hand wrote:

> The services must be trusted to determine what information may be broadcast without prejudice to the "national defense," and their consent to its dissemination is as much evidenced by what they do not seek to suppress, as by what they utter. Certainly it cannot be unlawful to spread such information within the United States; and, if so, it would be to the last degree fatuous to forbid its transmission to the citizens of a friendly foreign power.[14]

United States v. Scarbeck

The special statute[15] under which Scarbeck was indicted makes it a crime for an official to transfer to a foreign or communist agent any classified information. This provision is the only portion of the espionage laws geared directly to the classification system. As such, it permits a trial in which the government need not disclose the nature and significance of the information alleged to have been transferred. In *Scarbeck* there was oral testimony by the American Ambassador to Poland showing that the documents passed by Scarbeck to officials of the Polish government were marked with classification stamps, and that these stamps had been put on the documents by the Ambassador, who was authorized by executive order to classify documents. Nothing more, the court held, was required for a finding of guilt. Specifically, the propriety of the classification was not to be an issue in the case; and no showing of evil intent was required, beyond what could be inferred from the very identity of the recipients.[16]

Scarbeck suggests the possibility of a similar procedure in trials under sections 793 and 794. That is, the government might propose to establish, by simply asserting the mere fact of classification, that the information is "related to the national defense"—without the need to reveal the secrets that are in issue or to prove anything about how harmful their release would be. As far as prosecutions for leaking information to the public are concerned, it is not clear that this innovation would materially ease the government's burden of proof. Unless stamped official documents had changed hands, it would be difficult to prove that the particular information was in fact classified, much less to prove it was *known* by the accused to be classified. Yet to presume such guilty knowledge on the part of a criminal defendant would fly in the face of the presumption of innocence. In fact, we think such a procedure would be unconstitutional, despite the *Scarbeck* decision.

The application of *Scarbeck* procedures under the 1917 law seems precluded by the *Gorin* holding that it is for the jury to determine whether given information relates to the national defense. Thus instructions to the jury to ignore the classification markings on documents have been upheld in post-*Scarbeck* decisions.[17] The *Scarbeck* procedure has been accepted by the courts only in the context of a statute covering transfers of classified information to communist or foreign agents—a situation in which evil or reckless intent can plausibly be inferred even without a showing that the information was important. In the case of a statute that purported to punish all transfers of classified information without limitation as to the recipient, the danger of punishing truly innocent activity would be substantially greater. Such a law, we think, would meet constitutional requirements only if interpreted to mean that the government had to prove not only the fact of classification, but the propriety of the classification and the defendant's intent to injure the United States as well. Even then, the result would be less than satisfactory. The fact that the present executive order permits an item to be classified is simply not of much relevance to the underlying question: whether the national security would be seriously jeopardized by its release.

These cases and the relatively few others decided under the espionage laws settled only a few issues of statutory interpretation and constitutional law. Others, such as the meaning of the cryptic terms "unauthorized possession" and "not entitled to receive," would surface only when the government, for the first time, sought to use sections 793 (d) and (e) of the espionage statutes in a situation involving the public release of classified documents.

The Pentagon Papers Criminal Trial

The case of *United States* v. *Russo and Ellsberg* was dismissed by Judge Matthew Byrne in an unreported oral opinion, because of government misconduct.[18] The proceedings terminated before the Judge came to definite and final conclusions about interpretation of the espionage law. Nevertheless, Judge Byrne did issue a tentative statement at the beginning of the trial, and later he gave a number of instructions to the jury that were consistent with, and covered most of the points raised in, his preliminary interpretation.

Although some factual details were in dispute at the trial, the basic outline of what occurred was not in contest. In Chapter 2, we recounted the events that led to the production and disclosure of the Pentagon Papers. The FBI knew in the spring of 1970 that Ellsberg had copied the volumes and given them to Senator Fulbright, but no action was then taken against him. Subsequently, in June 1971, the *New York Times* and later the *Washington Post* began to publish excerpts from the Pentagon Papers. The civil action in which the government sought to enjoin such publication is discussed in Appendix B. On the eve of the Supreme Court decision in that case, Ellsberg was indicted for one count each of theft and espionage. Subsequently, he and Anthony Russo were reindicted on fifteen counts of espionage, conspiracy, and theft. The main espionage charges were lodged under sections 793(d) and (e).[19]

The indictment as handed down by the grand jury accused Ellsberg and Russo of violating either section 793(d) or section 793(e), which are virtually identical except that (d) deals with transmittals by a person in *authorized* possession of documents or information relating to the national defense, and (e) with acts done by one in *unauthorized* possession. At the trial the judge directed the government to choose between proceeding under section (d) or (e); that is, to determine whether it regarded Ellsberg as an authorized possessor or not. The government, for reasons that were never explained, opted for section (e), thereby taking on the added burden of proving that Ellsberg was in unauthorized possession of the Pentagon Papers.

In an apparent effort to avoid directly confronting the problems involved in punishing the transfer of information to Congress or to the press, the indictment was limited to the period of xeroxing. Ellsberg's main offense thus appeared to consist of permitting Anthony Russo (a person "not entitled to receive") to assist him in xeroxing a copy of the Pentagon Papers.[20] The government alleged that Ellsberg was not authorized to take the volumes off the premises of the Rand Corporation, nor even to keep them in his own safe at Rand, rather than in Rand's top secret facility; and that he was not authorized to give them to Russo or to others. No evidence was presented at the trial respecting the reason for the xeroxing or what was done with the xeroxed copies.

This was the first espionage indictment in American history that failed to allege that the defendants had the intent, or even the reason to believe, that the material would be used to the injury of the national defense or to the advantage of a foreign power. It was also the first case that did not involve the alleged transfer of information to foreign agents or spies.[21]

The defense attack on the indictment proceeded directly from the Supreme Court's decision in *Gorin*. (See pp. 111-112.) Without a requirement of *scienter*, the defense argued, the phrase "relating to the national defense" becomes vague and overbroad. The government stubbornly took the position that the broad *Gorin* definition of national defense information is acceptable even where the non-*scienter* provisions of the espionage statute are involved. In this the prosecution was implicitly bolstered by the fact that, as the defendants knew, the study was classified.

The court rejected the notion that any document known to be classified would automatically be "related to the national defense." In fact, Judge Byrne adopted the position that the fact of classification was not to be considered at all in determining whether information related to the national defense.[22]

However, the judge was unwilling to rule that the absence of a *scienter* requirement makes section 793(e) unconstitutional on its face. Instead, he found the requisite specificity in the language of that section itself, which refers to "information relating to the national defense which information the possessor has reason to believe could be used to the injury of the United States or to the advantage of any foreign nation." This qualification is not a *scienter* requirement; it points to an "objective" quality of the documents themselves rather than to a defendant's actual state of mind.

Now under Executive Order 10501, in effect at the relevant time, a document could be classified confidential if its disclosure "could be prejudicial to the defense interests of the United States." Thus the court's ruling came very close, in effect, to saying that information "relates to the national defense" if it is classifiable, whether or not actually classified.

Judge Byrne framed the issue as follows:

> Are the documents the type that require protection in the interests of national defense in that their disclosure could adversely affect or injure this nation or lead to the advantage of any foreign nation.[23]

Under the Supreme Court holding in *Gorin* that the question of relation to the national defense was a factual determination for the jury to make, Judge Byrne next ruled that the government was obliged to put into evidence the critical information alleged to meet the statutory test. Thus, the four negotiating volumes of the Pentagon Papers, which no one had made public prior to the trial, were put into evidence by the government and were available for reading and copying out by hand in the clerk's office.

At a number of stages during the presentation of evidence, Judge Byrne instructed the jury that it would be its job to determine from the documents and the testimony about them whether the information therein could have been used to injure the United States, or to give an advantage to a foreign power in connection with the defense of the United States. Under the circumstances the jury's task was a difficult one indeed. The government witnesses, principally Generals Paul Gorman and William DePuy, asserted that, *as a whole*, the information in the documents could have been used to the injury of the United States or to the advantage of a foreign power. While giving examples now and then, the prosecution refused to commit itself firmly as to which particular information they were referring to, and, indeed, continued to advocate the unmodified *Gorin* position, that virtually all the material "related to the national defense," and that no more need be shown.

The defense, forbidden to make the "irrelevant" argument that there was no criminal intent and that the documents were not given to a foreign power but to a senator, undertook to rebut the government's case by showing that there was no information in the volumes that could be used to the injury of the United States or to the advantage of a foreign power. Some of the defense witnesses testified about all of the volumes named in the indictment, and others about only one or two of them. They argued that neither the volumes as a whole nor any specific information in them met these requirements.

The impact of this testimony is a moot point, since the case never was submitted to the jury; yet jurors interviewed after the dismissal suggested that the government had failed to meet its burden of proof on this central issue.[24]

The defense argued further that if any of the information could be viewed as "relating to the national defense," its release still would not be culpable, for the information was already in the public domain. *Gorin* and *Heine* had approved this defense for the cases, respectively, of information released by the government and information that was at no time a secret.[25] But now, the court had to come to grips with a third situation: the documents in issue were indeed regarded as secret by the government, but the defense was prepared to show, for any given piece of information the government chose, that it might in fact have been found also, by a careful researcher, in documents of public record.

The defense argued that if the information appeared in the public domain in any form, transmitting that information could not be espionage. The government argued that as long as the information was obtained from documents that the government was keeping secret, there could be no public domain defense. On this question, the court accepted the position of the defense completely. The court permitted the introduction of a great deal of evidence offered to show that information in the documents, and particularly information to which the government witnesses had pointed as specifically "related to the national defense," was already in the public domain. In some cases, the defense was able to show that the information had been put into the public domain by the government; in other cases, they could show only that it had been printed in publicly available documents.[26]

"Related to the national defense" is by no means the only problematic expression in the espionage laws. Section 793 (e) of the espionage act contains two other exceedingly cryptic phrases: "unauthorized possession" and "not entitled to receive." There is nothing in the statute, and not much in the legislative history or prior court decisions, to indicate how one would determine who was in "unauthorized possession" of a document related to the national defense, or who was "not entitled to receive" such a document.

In no earlier case had the government alleged unauthorized possession on the part of a government official or other person who had a security clearance. Moreover, in this case there was testimony, uncontested by the government, that access was authorized for Ellsberg by the president and vice president of the Rand Corporation in accordance with Department of Defense procedures, as well as by those who had deposited the Pentagon Papers at Rand. The defense argued that this authorization disposed of the issue. The government contended that Ellsberg's possession of the documents, although initially authorized, had later become unauthorized by virtue of what he had done with them. The documents, the government argued, were classified, and hence were subject to the rules established by the President's executive order, as well as the rules found in documents known as the Industrial Security Manual and the Rand Corporation manual, both of which apply to officials and employees of the Rand Corporation.[27] Under these rules, Ellsberg was not authorized to take the documents out of Rand Corporation premises to xerox them, nor to show them to Russo. These actions, the government argued, made Ellsberg's possession of the documents unauthorized. In effect, proof of violation of the manuals would *ipso facto* prove unauthorized possession of the documents.

The statute first introduced in Congress in 1917 had specifically authorized the President to determine which individuals were "entitled to receive" material related to the national defense. Without explanation this provision was removed from the bill during the Senate-House conference; no substitute procedure was provided for determining who was "entitled to receive."[28] In earlier trials this oversight had caused little difficulty. When Judith Coplon was accused of giving documents to an agent of the Soviet Government, the defense conceded that the Soviet agent was a person "not entitled to receive" the documents within the meaning of the statute. In the present case, the defense argued that the only constitutionally acceptable definition of one "not entitled to receive" was a person who could be expected to use the information to injure the United States or to give advantage to a foreign power. Thus any loyal citizen, and certainly a member of Congress, is "entitled to receive" information. For this issue, the government again relied upon the rules of the classification system: A person was "not entitled to receive" unless he had both a security clearance and an official duty in connection with the documents.

The government's attempt to rely on the classification system here raised the most grave questions of overbreadth, improper delegation and lack of notice. The defense argued that the executive order and the manuals could not fairly be used to interpret the criminal statute. The statute itself gave no fair warning that its meaning was to be so interpreted. Likewise, the executive order on classification was designed to establish administrative procedures for the storage and handling of classified information within the government; nowhere did it clearly identify itself as implementing or interpreting the espionage statute. Nowhere in the executive order was "unauthorized possession" defined; the executive order did not even use the term, "not entitled to receive."

The Security Manuals were no more satisfactory in terms of definitional clarity. Moreover, even if the President could be, and had in fact been authorized by Congress to define what shall be a crime, it did not follow that the Rand Corporation could lawfully do so.

Over the strenuous objections of the defense, the court permitted the introduction of the Industrial Security Manual and the Rand Security Manual. By this ruling, the relevance of the classification system was apparently recognized in principle. Yet the court stressed to the jury that the manuals did not define the espionage law or any of its terms as such; the rationale for admitting them was not made entirely clear.[29]

A further ruling controlled the impact of the classification system on the case: the court would require the government to prove that the documents were properly classified, both in a procedural and in a substantive sense. That is, if they wished to rely on the classification structure to prove unauthorized possession (or any other element of an offense), the government would have to show not only that the documents were classified by someone with authority to classify them, following the prescribed procedures, but also that the documents were "in fact classifiable—that is, at a minimum did they contain informational material, the unauthorized disclosure of which would be prejudicial to the defense interests of the United States."[30]

This heavy burden the prosecution never attempted directly to meet. In lieu of proving that prescribed classification procedures had been followed, the prosecution apparently intended to rely on a presumption of administrative regularity. Nor did the prosecution offer any evidence that the documents were classifiable, beyond the assertions, discussed above, that as a whole they could be of use to a foreign power. Defense witnesses, on the other hand, testified that the documents could not at the time of the alleged offenses have been properly classified "confidential."

Whatever might have been the impact of the court's rulings on the outcome of this particular case, the partial and equivocal recognition afforded to the classification system seems highly unsatisfactory in principle. While the 1950 statute involved in *Scarbeck* (see pp. 113-114) is expressly keyed to the classification system, Congress has refrained from amending the 1917 law to incorporate the same approach. Thus the court's rulings in the Ellsberg-Russo trial seem inconsistent with the legislative intent.

Even more important, the court failed to deal forthrightly with the powerful constitutional arguments raised by the defense. No definitive ruling was made on these arguments prior to the termination of the case because of government misconduct. The dismissal left the government free to bring further prosecutions for the well-intended release of information to Congress or the public. An official or other citizen contemplating such action must now anticipate a potential trial focusing primarily on the single question of whether the information *could* be used to injure the United States or give advantage to a foreign power. Where information is current, unlike the historical material contained in the Pentagon Papers, it will be difficult to argue that the information could not be used in any way to injure the United States or to give aid to a foreign power. It is no answer to point out that the government has the burden of proof beyond a reasonable doubt; for the overriding question, whether the need for publicity is not paramount, is entirely suppressed by this formulation of the issue. Even allowing for the proper reluctance of trial judges to hold statutes unconstitutional, that a conscientious judge felt obliged to meet halfway the outrageous claims advanced by the government is testimony to the need for legislative initiatives to clarify the espionage laws.

Appendix B

Prior Restraint

The First Amendment was designed to bar prior censorship of political expression. Prior censorship has traditionally been seen as the most odious form of interference with free speech, because of its direct impact on the interests of the audience as well as those of the speaker. Of course, the precise application of this principle is open to dispute; and some of the more important ambiguities have scarcely been litigated. The Supreme Court has never ruled that citizens have an affirmative, constitutional right of access to governmental information. On the other hand, the Court has never upheld an injunction against publication of political information. Such a drastic measure, potentially enforceable by the confiscation of printed matter and by summary contempt proceedings, has seldom recommended itself even to the executive branch. Indeed, the Nixon administration's attempt to enjoin publication of the Pentagon Papers was the first case of its kind.

The precedent available to the Court in that case grew out of attempts, usually by state and local authorities, to regulate far different speech activities, such as meetings, demonstrations, and door-to-door canvasing or propaganda campaigns. In evaluating such regulations, the Court's approach had been to inquire, first, whether the threatened evil—usually violence or other disruption of

125

normal activity—was sufficiently grave, immediate, and definite to justify interference with the "compelling interest" protected by the First Amendment; and second, whether the proposed regulation was both rationally related to the end in view and sufficiently restricted in scope to avoid unnecessary interference with protected activity.

In general, the Court had given great but not conclusive weight to governmental findings of fact and judgments of policy, especially where both the legislative and the executive branch had concurred in such findings or judgments. The strictest possible scrutiny had been given to unilateral executive actions, supported only by a claim of inherent power, that sought to limit the fundamental rights of citizens. Even where an Act of Congress was in question, however, the Court had not hesitated to demand a persuasive showing that the circumstances truly justified the particular measure in view.[1]

In the Pentagon Papers case, the government began in the lower courts by arguing that the President's power derived from the espionage laws, but by the time the matter reached the Supreme Court, the government was basing its position entirely on the inherent powers of the President.[2]

The government's case was further weakened by the circumstances of the litigation. Its attorneys proved to be poorly acquainted with the contents of the Papers, and the government's case rested in part on a sealed brief that could not be discussed in open court.

It is therefore not surprising that the Court ultimately rejected the government's plea for injunctions against the *New York Times* and the *Washington Post*. The Court voted six to three that the government was not entitled to an injunction against either newspaper. Still, for 17 days, from June 14 to June 30, the *New York Times* had been restrained by a court order from publishing material in its possession. The temporary restraint was flatly disapproved by Justices Black and Douglas, in view of their position that the constitutional ban against prior restraint is absolute. However, a clear majority of the Supreme Court considered prior restraint permissible under some circumstances and held that a restraining order was therefore appropriate pending evaluation of the substantive issues.

The Supreme Court's unsigned *per curiam* opinion, representing the domain of agreement among the six majority justices, was breathtakingly short. Its substantive discussion read as follows:

"Any system of prior restraints of expression comes to this Court bearing a heavy presumption against its constitutional validity." Bantam Books, Inc. v. Sullivan, 372 U.S. 58, 70 (1963); see also Near v. Minnesota, 283 U.S. 697 (1931). The government "thus carries a heavy burden of showing justification for the enforcement of such a restraint." Organization for a Better Austin v. Keefe, 402 U.S. 415 (1971). The District Court for the Southern District of New York in the *New York Times* case and the District Court for the District of Columbia and the Court of Appeals for the District of Columbia Circuit in the *Washington Post* case held that the government had not met that burden. We agree.[3]

Each of the six majority Justices—Black, Douglas, Brennan, Stewart, White, and Marshall—expounded his individual views in a separate concurring opinion.

Justice Black approached the case on the basis of his "absolutist" view of the First Amendment, under which no limitations can be put on protected speech. Declaring that "every moment's continuation of the injunction against these newspapers amounts to a flagrant, indefensible, and continuing violation of the First Amendment," he argued that the restraining order against the *Times* should have been vacated without argument. "No one," he went on, "can read the history of the adoption of the First Amendment without being convinced beyond any doubt that it was injunctions like these sought here that Madison and his collaborators intended to outlaw in this nation for all time."

Only Justice Douglas was willing to agree with this absolutist position.[4] While joining in Justice Black's opinion, Justice Douglas also wrote a separate opinion, in which Justice Black concurred, presenting a supplemental or fallback position. Striking at the heart of the inherent powers argument, Justice Douglas emphasized that in the espionage laws, Congress had deliberately refrained from making criminal the "publication" of information related to the national defense. Because prior restraints are even more offensive to First

Amendment values than are criminal penalties, the congressional judgment severely undercut the position of the executive branch. In the face of this indication of a contrary legislative policy, Justice Douglas concluded that the Court could not issue an injunction against publication.

Other Justices were equally unimpressed with the logic of inherent powers, and were therefore concerned to discover the intent of Congress. Justices White and Stewart, each of whom concurred in the other's separate opinion, were inclined to believe that section 793 (e) of the espionage laws does apply to "publication," as well as to "communication," of information related to the national defense. While disagreeing with Justice Douglas on this point, however, they did not find the espionage law supportive of the government's injunction suit. Quite the contrary, they held it devastating to the government's case that Congress had specifically addressed the problem but had chosen only to establish criminal sanctions and had failed to provide for injunctive authority.[5] As in the *Steel Seizure Case*,[6] where legislation defined the exclusive means to deal with labor disputes in defense plants, Congress had in the espionage laws provided an exclusive remedy for unauthorized disclosures of information. Without a very special showing of exigency, at least, these Justices held it was not proper for the other branches to add injunctive power to the criminal penalties established by Congress.

Combining the thrust of these several analyses, Justice Marshall found it unnecessary to determine the scope of the espionage laws. Pointing out that the government had not committed itself as to whether the act of publication was a crime, he concluded that the injunction should be denied in either case. If Congress had not made publication a crime, then there was no legislative determination of grave danger, such as would be required to support an injunction. On the other hand if Congress had made the action a crime, this placed the executive branch in possession of a sufficient, constitutionally preferable, alternative means of dealing with unauthorized disclosures.

Justice Brennan, like Justice Black, did not discuss the intent of Congress. He urged that even a temporary restraining order should not be issued unless the court was convinced beyond a doubt that there would be "inevitably, directly, and immediately . . . irreparable damage to our nation or its people." The government, he added, must not submit a mere conclusion that such harm would result, but must make available sufficient supporting evidence for judicial scrutiny.

Each of the three dissenters also wrote a separate opinion. Justice Harlan's dissent, which Justices Burger and Blackmun joined, did not focus on the absence of congressional authorization for prior restraints. Instead, like Justice Brennan, he addressed himself directly to the question of the proper standard for judicial review. Justice Harlan argued that the judiciary's role where foreign policy or national defense questions were concerned is a very limited one: It must accord the greatest deference to a bona fide determination by the relevant agency head that disclosure "would irreparably impair the nation's security."

While he criticized the lower courts for failing to adhere to this standard of self-restraint, Justice Harlan concluded that the case could not be properly decided without further development of a number of issues.[7]

The dissenting opinions of Justices Burger and Blackmun stressed their discomfort at the unseemly pace of the litigation, the fragmentary nature of the factual record, and the poverty of applicable legal standards. They concluded that the cases should be remanded for further hearings. Chief Justice Burger addressed himself in passing to the issue of inherent powers, suggesting that in his view the absence of congressional support was not especially damaging to the government's case.

This review of the separate opinions filed by the Justices suggests that the Court's position can be characterized as proceeding from four basic propositions:

—rejection of the view that prior restraints are never permissible;

—rejection of the view that it lies solely with the executive branch to determine the need for prior restraints in any given case;

—recognition of the powerful, but not conclusive, weight of congressional judgment in determining when prior restraint is permissible;

—insistence on the power of the judiciary to make its own judgment, founded on adequate evidence and argument, as to what the law is.[8]

It appears that the Court is most reluctant to validate prior restraints that lack an explicit congressional mandate, save possibly in the most uniquely pressing and grave emergency. Justice Brennan characterized the limiting case as one where the government could prove, with cogent evidence, that publication must "inevitably, directly and immediately" cause a harm equivalent in magnitude to a wartime disclosure imperiling the safety of American troops. Justice Stewart stated that in the absence of express congressional authorization, speech might be enjoined if it would "surely result in direct, immediate, and irreparable damage to our Nation or its people." We may take these standards as a straightforward gloss on the less specific language of the *per curiam* opinion: that any proposal for prior restraint comes to court with a very heavy presumption against it.

Of course, if a generalized prior restraint statute were enacted, the Court would still have an obligation to determine its constitutionality, and the measure would still come to court "bearing a heavy presumption against its constitutional validity."

The Court's treatment of this case reflects the spirit of caution that governs its approach to decisions affecting national security. The most serious criticism, we think, would be that in its attempt to avoid creating bad law, the Court created a good deal more uncertainty than was necessary. The prospect of becoming involved in costly and controversial litigation must have a deeply chilling effect on the calculations of would-be publishers, even if the chance of a final decision in favor of the government is regarded as very unlikely.

Having shunned the absolutist view, for better or for worse, the Court was obliged to somehow balance the competing interests involved. Yet this was done in an exceedingly uninformative manner. The critical part of the government's case was not presented or weighed in public; the court entertained *in camera* the government's showing of threatened harm, though at least the opposing parties were allowed to study that showing. In contrast, the explicit case against prior restraint rested only on the presumptive legal force of the First Amendment. Because the government failed to overcome that presumption, the Court did not need to discuss explicitly the concrete public interest in disclosure of the Pentagon Papers. Thus the public record of this litigation offered precious little guidance for the disposition of future prior restraint cases. The resulting ambiguity has proved unfortunate.

The Marchetti Case

While the government did not prevail in the Pentagon Papers case, the lacunae in the various concurring opinions encouraged further attempts at prior restraint. The case of Victor Marchetti shortly produced the first—and so far the only—successful suit to enjoin political speech in the United States.[9] This departure has received remarkably little notice in the press and the learned journals of the legal profession.

The facts of the case may be stated briefly. Victor Marchetti spent some 14 years with the CIA, rising to the level of staff assistant in the offices of the Director and the Deputy Director. After retiring in 1969, Marchetti decided to write a nonfictional account of CIA operations, particularly its covert intelligence gathering and covert political activities. An article and an outline for a larger study that he submitted to several publishers were forwarded to the CIA by a publisher's employee. Without contacting Marchetti, the agency went into court in the Eastern District of Virginia with a secret affidavit from its Deputy Director for Operations, Thomas H. Karamessines. That very day, on April 18, 1972, Judge Bryan granted a temporary restraining order prohibiting Marchetti from disclosing without CIA approval any information that he had learned by reason of his employment that related to intelligence activities, sources, or methods, except information subsequently disclosed by the United States. On May 19, 1972, Judge Bryan issued a permanent injunction, holding that Marchetti had waived his First Amendment rights when he went to work for the government, and again at the termination of his employment, by signing statements promising not to reveal classified information or information relating to intelligence matters.

On appeal, the Fourth Circuit Court of Appeals affirmed Judge Bryan's decision. They found the secrecy agreement a reasonable exercise of the President's power as commander-in-chief, and they pointed to the director's statutory mandate to preserve the secrets of intelligence sources and methods.[10] This power could be exercised, they suggested, not merely to prevent "grave and irreparable harm" but whenever "disclosure may reasonably be thought to be inconsistent with the national interest."[11] However, they modified the injunction in one respect: It would apply only to *classified* intelligence information and not to all intelligence information. The court assumed that the CIA would simply determine which information was classified, and that ordinarily no serious controversy about this could arise. This assumption proved grossly unfounded.

When Marchetti, now working with John Marks, completed his manuscript, it was duly submitted to the CIA, which originally ordered some 399 deletions. Of these demands, all save 168 were dropped after negotiations. Mr. Marchetti and Mr. Marks, joined by their publisher, Knopf, were entitled under the Fourth Circuit's decision to dispute in court the government's assertion that the 168 still contested items were classified, and that they had not entered the public domain. Thus a second round of litigation began.

As the plaintiffs were quick to point out, the fact that information is contained in a stamped document does not prove that the particular piece of information was classified, or even classifiable. Under the rules of the classification system, every page in a document is to be stamped when any one sentence on any one page of it gets classified. Thus, many unclassified sentences appear on pages stamped at top and bottom.

Plaintiffs conceded that a few of the documents submitted by the government were marked in such a specific way that they did show that an authorized official had classified a contested item during the period of Marks's or Marchetti's access to the information. Based on the written evidence, the court accepted as classified only a few items besides those conceded by the plaintiffs. In all, only 28 of the deletions demanded by the CIA were proven to the court's satisfaction to be classified.

The Fourth Circuit had overlooked the fact that the classification procedures are designed, as they must be, to control the storage and dissemination of documents. The documents do not, and could not, reveal the classification status of bits of information.

The litigation had proceeded so far on the assumption that, under *EPA* v. *Mink*, [12] the courts were not to inquire whether classified information was properly classified; instead the mere fact of classification would be treated as conclusive against disclosure. Thus the controversy in the district court related primarily to whether the disputed items were in fact classified. As the Fourth Circuit, rehearing the case on appeal, now recognized, the new Freedom of Information Act had overturned the doctrine of *Mink*: Under the new act any citizen could now contest the propriety of the classification in question. It followed that the present plaintiffs must also be entitled to contest that issue, since "these plaintiffs should not be denied the right to publish information which any citizen could compel the CIA to produce and, after production, could publish."[13]

On the other hand, the Court of Appeals saw little merit in the district court's treatment of the classification question. While it had proved unexpectedly difficult for the government to prove that a specific item had in fact been deliberately classified, the relevance of such proof for the ultimate issues was obscure. If the deleted items were truly sensitive, a procedural irregularity on the agency's part would not soften the implications for national security of a court-ordered disclosure. The Fourth Circuit determined, therefore, that all the classifiable information in a stamped document should ordinarily be presumed classified.[14]

The Court of Appeals went on to approve the ruling of the court below, that the public domain defense applies only to information officially released. They reasoned that even if rumors had already reached the public concerning a certain matter, confirmation of rumors by one in Marchetti's position could cause further harm to the national interest.

The court concluded by remanding the case to the trial court, where the issue of classifiability could now be litigated. When plaintiffs declined to request a trial on that issue, the district court issued a final order denying release of the disputed materials. Thus the litigation came to an end in October 1975, leaving in effect the permanent injunction issued in May 1972. The book was published with 168 items deleted by government order.[15]

Not only is there no textual authority for prior restraints on speech, but there is of course a constitutional provision that seems flatly to proscribe them. Yet in upholding the first judicially sanctioned prior restraint in our nation's history, the court pronounced the First Amendment irrelevant to the case. This curious conclusion was held to result from the operation of Marchetti's secrecy agreement, but the court failed to recognize that the force and effect of such an agreement must itself be determined in the light of First Amendment standards. The court thus assumed away the First Amendment rights not only of Marchetti himself, but of his publisher and the general public as well.

Three further considerations make the emphasis the court placed on the secrecy agreement seem even more inappropriate. First, the court stated that even without an explicit contract, a binding commitment not to reveal government secrets was implicit in Marchetti's acceptance of his employment. Second, even if there had been justification for characterizing the litigation as simply a contracts case, the court itself abandoned that position when it recognized the relevance of the Freedom of Information Act. If Marchetti's employment contract did not impair his rights, or those of the public, to obtain information under the FOIA, it would seem to follow *a fortiori* that the contract could not impair his or third parties' rights under the First Amendment either.[16]

Third, and most important, is the court's failure to recognize that Congress has expressed its policy judgment by steadfastly refusing to authorize prior restraints. The *Marchetti* court contrived to sidestep this issue by reasoning that the secrecy agreement disposed of the First Amendment aspect of the case. But this reasoning was circular and unpersuasive.

The power of the executive branch to limit speech as a condition of the employment contract is not based on express statutory authority. Like the classification system, it rests on the President's roles as commander-in-chief and as head of the civilian bureaucracy. These duties Congress has left, within broad limits, to executive discretion, though some limits are set by legislation. The law[17] that authorizes the CIA Director to protect intelligence sources and methods refers to no specific means. However it is clear that the CIA was not intended to exercise internal police functions, even vis-à-vis agents of foreign powers operating within the United States. This law can be fairly read to contemplate reasonable administrative precautions only; it authorizes judicially sanctioned prior restraints no more than it does kidnapping, burglary, or homicides. Congress never foresaw any conflict between this provision and First Amendment values; that the courts will look for more specific congressional authority when First Amendment rights are strongly implicated is shown by such cases as *Green* v. *McElroy*[18] involving arbitrary withdrawal of a security clearance.

Justice Jackson's concurring opinion in the *Steel Seizure Case* presented the argument that the validity of presidential acts and judgments depends on their relationship to those of Congress, and he distinguished three situations for analysis:

> 1. When the President acts pursuant to an expressed or implied authorization of Congress, his authority is at its maximum, for it includes all that he possesses in his own right plus all that Congress can delegate . . .
>
> 2. When the President acts in absence of either a congressional grant or denial of authority, he can only rely upon his own independent powers . . .
>
> 3. When the President takes measures incompatible with the express or implied will of Congress, his power is at his lowest ebb, for then he can rely only on his own constitutional powers minus any constitutional powers of Congress over the matter.[19]

A President's attempts at prior restraint on publication fall squarely in the third category. Congress has not given the executive branch general authority to seek injunctions on publication; on the contrary, it has repeatedly refused to do so.

In 1917 President Wilson proposed an amendment to the espionage laws that appeared to sanction injunctions against publication. Congress rejected this proposal.[20] In 1950, when Congress undertook revision of the Internal Security Act, including various amendments to the espionage laws, it added a sentence specifically providing that nothing in the act should be taken to imply authority for prior restraints on publication.[21] Congress has, however, legislated one very narrow authorization for prior restraint. In the Atomic Energy Act, Congress provided in 1954 that the executive branch could seek an injunction against violations of the criminal provisions of that Act.[22]

Congress has carefully chosen specific regulatory techniques and sanctions to meet specific problems. It authorized prior restraint only in this one instance; and the utterances sought to be restrained in *Marchetti* were not alleged to be within that area of specifically authorized prior restraint. In fact, both the absence of congressional authority for prior restraints and the need for such authority have been implicitly recognized by the executive branch, in that it developed a proposal for legislation that would explicitly authorize injunctions on publication of intelligence information.[23]

The technique relied on most heavily by Congress to protect national security information has been the threat of criminal sanctions. Yet even here Congress has also adhered to a highly cautious, selective approach.[24]

The Court in the *Pentagon Papers* case left unresolved the question whether the general espionage laws could be stretched to cover any disclosure of classified information to the American people, done without intent to injure the United States. We argued in Appendix A that they cannot be so applied; for present purposes it suffices to point out that, as Justice Marshall showed in the *Pentagon Papers* case, the relevance of the criminal laws for establishing injunction authority is far from clear. On the analysis of Justice Jackson in the *Steel Seizure* case, passage of such a law would actually weaken the legal basis for any other remedy not expressly authorized. This result is especially appropriate in the present context, because prior restraints are more offensive to First Amendment values than is criminal punishment.

The constitutional objections to prior restraint would be formidable even if it were clearly authorized by Congress; and they attain maximum force where it is not. The Supreme Court in the *Pentagon Papers* case responded to the absence of congressional authorization by requiring (as Justices Brennan and Stewart put it) proof that direct, immediate, and irreparable damage would flow from failure to act. By no stretch of the imagination can the *Marchetti* decision be reconciled with this requirement. The Fourth Circuit required no showing of impending harm, beyond the bare fact that the information meets the executive order's test for "confidential" classification—that disclosure could reasonably be expected to harm the national security. This standard may be appropriate in Freedom of Information Act cases; it is not so where the government, in the face of the First Amendment and without statutory sanction, seeks to impose a prior restraint on the process of public debate.

If the substantive standard applied in *Marchetti* was inconsistent with First Amendment values, the procedure employed was also utterly alien to traditional due process concepts, which call for adversary representation and an open weighing of the evidence of both sides. The original temporary restraining order against Marchetti was issued on the basis of a secret government brief, evaluated by the court in an *ex parte* hearing with only the government side represented.

We cannot satisfy ourselves that the court correctly evaluated the actual degree of exigency in this particular case, because the information in question is still secret. We are entitled to be skeptical, however, for it is clear beyond doubt that under the present executive order there is much properly classified information, the release of which would not gravely harm the nation but would make a definite contribution to legitimate public debate. Moreover, experience does indicate the extent to which cries of alarm by the executive can be inflated. As to the Pentagon Papers, the government argued unsuccessfully in five different courts that publication could be disastrous. Several Supreme Court Justices were evidently convinced, but felt that the First Amendment made an injunction legally improper all the same. In the aftermath of the publication of the Papers, it is difficult to identify any such damage. Indeed, executive officials have admitted that the alarms were raised in court in order to gain time to study the Papers and before any persuasive judgment of danger could conceivably have been made.[25]

Publication in June 1974 of Marchetti's book, including many once "classified" items which the CIA had originally wished to have deleted, has so far caused no visible damage either. Certainly, none of the disclosures threatens any "grave and irreparable harm" to the national defense. The courts in this case, however, have not only taken at face value the government's evaluation of risk, but have adopted procedures that hinder the presentation of conflicting evidence. Once again, the issue of the value of disclosure for legitimate public debate is entirely suppressed. This, we think, is intolerable.

A final objection to the result in *Marchetti* flows from the doctrine that a restriction on political speech must be restricted to the narrowest possible scope, in order to minimize its interference with protected activity. The injunction now in effect applies to all classified information not officially released, and the requirement of prior CIA censorship for all Marchetti's intelligence-related public speech is flagrantly over-broad. We believe that such a measure would be unconstitutional even if expressly authorized by Congress.

The issue, after all, is not merely whether the government may elicit from employees a promise to respect its legitimate secrets, or whether one who reveals such secrets may be denied access to sensitive materials, dismissed from his position, or even conceivably sued for damages. The issue is one of prior restraints affecting not only the official's right to speak but the right of Congress and the people to know. Such considerations cannot be avoided by pointing to a "contract." Prior restraints, whether directed to officials or otherwise, have not been authorized by law. Such a law would in any event bear a heavy presumption of invalidity. And what applies to the attempt to restrain publication of a specific document, surely applies *a fortiori* to the attempt to subject an individual to a permanent regime of censorship with only the flimsiest of procedural safeguards.

From a legal point of view, the recent attempts at prior restraint run counter to our traditional understanding of the First Amendment and also to the consistent policy of Congress. Viewed politically, these attempts tend to serve the purposes of the secrecy system rather than those of the nation as a whole. They point to the objective of a bureaucratic utopia, in which prior restraints would automatically be available for the protection of any classified information. Even if the classification system were administered in the most scrupulous manner, the fact that a document was classified would not necessarily mean that its release would seriously damage the national security. Under present conditions, it is clear that much information is classified precisely because of its potential value to Congress and the public.

The courts' opinions in the *Pentagon Papers* and *Marchetti* cases have not reflected the sort of healthy skepticism that these considerations would justify. Even Justice Stewart's ostensibly strict test of "direct, immediate, and irreparable damage" may well lead sooner or later to grave abuses, especially if the courts do not insist on a most persuasive showing, under fair adversary procedures, before issuing even a temporary restraining order.

It may well be that the Founding Fathers meant to prohibit prior restraints absolutely. Whether or not this is so, the nation has managed quite well without them in the past. We believe that recent events, far from demonstrating a compelling need for new restraints on public debate, call for a renewed commitment to First Amendment values.

At the very least, we would argue that prior restraint becomes tolerable—if it ever does—only where Congress has expressly identified a specific type of information as requiring this utmost degree of protection. So far Congress has made such a finding only for atomic secrets, and this narrow provision for prior restraints has never been tested in court, because no occasion has arisen to use it.

We do not believe that a persuasive legal or political case has been made on behalf of further legislation of this type. Rather than enacting broader authority for prior restraints, Congress should reaffirm its historic opposition to such measures.

Notes

Chapter 2

1. Pentagon Papers Trial transcript (copies on file in the Harvard University Law Library).

United States-Vietnam Relations 1945-67, Department of Defense Study (for House Committee on Armed Services), 12 Vol., 1971. This official version omits certain material included in the Gravel and New York Times editions.

The Pentagon Papers, Senator Gravel Edition, (Boston: Beacon Press, Vol. 1-4, 1971).

The Pentagon Papers, New York Times, (New York: Quadrangle Books, 1971, hardcover; Bantam Books, 1971, softcover).

Peter Schrag, *Test of Loyalty,* (New York: Simon & Schuster, 1974).

Sanford J. Ungar, *The Papers & The Papers,* (New York: E.P. Dutton & Co., Inc. 1972).

The New York Times Company v. *United States,* The Pentagon Papers Litigation, Arno Press, 2 vols., 1971.

White House Surveillance Activities and Campaign Activities, Book VII, Parts 1-4, Impeachment Investigation, House Comm. on the Judiciary, 93d Cong., 2d Sess. (1974).

2. These "negotiating" volumes have yet to be published in their entirety, although considerable information from them has become public. In the course of the Ellsberg-Russo trial, discussed below, the government made use of some parts of the Pentagon Papers that had not previously been released, including the four "negotiating" volumes. These were introduced in evidence and were available to the public for copying in the office of the clerk. Nevertheless, after the trial the government still refused to make these volumes available to Senator Fulbright or to publish them. In 1975 the government released some 80 percent of their content in response to requests under the Freedom of Information Act, and they released most of the rest in 1977 in response to a civil suit brought under the act.

3. To anticipate the argument in Chapter 5, there was no information in the study that would be presumptively classified in our proposed system.

4. The others listed to receive copies were Henry Kissinger, the LBJ Library, JFK Library, and the DOD Archives. See the Statement of Information Submitted on Behalf of President Nixon, Hearings, Committee on the Judiciary, House of

141

Representatives, 93d Cong., 2d Sess., Book IV, White House Surveillance Activities, p. 118.

5. We discuss the legal issues involved in prior restraint cases in Appendix B.

6. See citations in note 1, this chapter.

7. Some of the legal issues in the Ellsberg trial are discussed in detail in Appendix A.

8. Bombing of Cambodia, Book XI, from the Impeachment Investigation (Richard M. Nixon), Statement of Information, House Committee on the Judiciary, 93d Cong., 2d. Sess. (1974).

Impeachment of Richard M. Nixon, President of the United States, Report, Committee on the Judiciary House of Representatives, 93d Cong., 2d Sess. (1974), pp. 217-219.

Bombing in Cambodia, Hearings, Senate Committee on Armed Services, 93d Cong., 1st Sess. (1973).

Press Conference of Melvin Laird (Jan. 29, 1974), reprinted in White House Surveillance Activities and Campaign Activities, Book VII-Part 1, Statement of Information, from Impeachment Investigation, House Comm. on the Judiciary, 93d Cong., 2d Sess. (1974), pp. 298-300.

Marvin & Bernard Kalb, *Kissinger* (Boston: Little Brown & Co. 1974).

9. Air War Against North Vietnam, Hearings, Senate Committee on Armed Services, 90th Cong., 1st Sess., Parts 1-5 (1967).

10. Presidential Documents 577.

11. The best discussions of the seventeen wiretaps of newsmen and government officials and of the more general subject of national security wiretaps are to be found in the House Committee on the Judiciary's Impeachment Inquiry Report, Minority Memorandum of Facts and Law, White House Surveillance Activities and Campaign Activities, Statement of Information, Book VII, Parts 1-4, Impeachment Investigation, House Comm. on the Judiciary, 93d Cong. 2d Sess. (1974); and in David Wise, *The American Police State,* New York: Random House, (1976), pp. 31-106. The legal issues raised by the taps are largely beyond the scope of this study.

12. Impeachment of Richard M. Nixon, Report No. 93-1305, House Judiciary Committee, 93d Cong., 2d Sess., pp. 218-19 (1974).

13. For fuller background on the Angola episode, see *CIA's Secret War in Angola,* Intelligence Report, Vol. I, No. I (Center for National Security Studies, 1975); Hearings before the Senate Select Committee on Intelligence Activity, 94th Cong., 1st Sess., Nov. 20, 1975; Hearings before the House Committee on Foreign Affairs, Subcommittee on Africa, 93d Cong., 2d Sess., March 14 & Oct. 8, 9, & 22, 1974; Hearings before the Senate Committee on Foreign Relations, Nomination of Nathaniel Davis, 94th Cong., 1st Sess., Feb. 19, 1975.

Chapter 3

1. For more detailed treatment of the history of the secrecy system, the reader may wish to consult J. R. Wiggins, *Freedom or Secrecy* (New York: Oxford Press, 1964); David Wise, *The Politics of Lying* (New York: Random House, 1973); and A. M. Schlesinger, Jr., *The Imperial Presidency* (Boston: Houghton, Mifflin, 1973).

2. Deposition of Richard Nixon at p. 13, *Halperin v. Kissinger,* Civ. Action No. 1187-73 (D.D.C. 1976).

3. See Chapter 4, n. 26.

4. Transcript of White House transcripts, July 24, 1971, reprinted in Statement of

Information, House Judiciary Committee, Impeachment Inquiry, Book VII, Part 2, pp. 874-79.

5. The propriety of such investigations and the question of what reforms might be instituted is beyond the scope of this study.

6. The Ford administration in February 1976 proposed legislation making it a crime for a present or former official to release information related to intelligence sources or methods, and authorizing the courts to enjoin disclosure of such information. See Message to Congress, Feb. 18, 1976, cited in Weekly Compilation of Presidential Documents; H.R. 12006, Feb. 19, 1976, 94th Cong., 2d Sess. Earlier, the Ford administration had endorsed even more sweeping proposals that would make it a crime for any person to disclose any classified information.

7. One might even go so far as to suggest that, in essence, bureaucracy is a veil of tiers.

8. The military services, for example, typically conceive of the national security interest in terms of their own struggle for greater budgets, prestige, and freedom of action. They do not try to economize in the expenditure of public funds or to help the legislature accomplish anything else. Thus the dominant element in the air force is primarily concerned with maximizing the flying combat capability of that service. It is left to others to determine how this objective relates to broader goals of nuclear deterrence, overall fighting capability, disarmament, and peace. See Morton H. Halperin, *Bureaucratic Politics and Foreign Policy*, (Washington, D.C.: Brookings, 1974), pp. 28-32.

9. Separate multiple independent reentry vehicle: a missile carrying several warheads that can strike targets.

10. For a discussion of the use and motives of leaks in detail see Morton Halperin, *Bureaucratic Politics and Foreign Policy;* and Leon V. Sigal, *Reporters and Officials: The Organization and Politics of Newsmaking* (Boston; D.C. Heath, 1953).

11. Seymour Hersh, "CIA Salvage Ship Brought Up Part of Soviet Sub Lost in 1968, Failed to Raise Atom Missiles," *New York Times,* March 19, 1975, Vol. CXXIV; Morton Kondracke, "The CIA and Our Conspiracy," [*MORE*], Vol. 5, No. 5, May 1975, p. 10.

12. Such tactics can be extremely esoteric, particularly when carried on at the White House level. For a discussion of this phenomenon, see Morton H. Halperin, *Bureaucratic Politics and Foreign Policy,* pp. 177-179.

13. When former Secretary of State Dean Rusk was asked whether any truly serious leaks had occurred during his tenure, he pointed to an incident during the Cuban missile crisis, in which his own unguarded expression of relief—"We are eyeball to eyeball and I think the other fellow just blinked"—had been revealed. Even granting that the leak was serious, this kind of remark is not the sort of information that a formal security classification system can be expected to protect. See Warrantless Wiretapping and Electronic Surveillance—1974, Joint Hearings before Senate Sub-Committees of Judiciary and Foreign Relations Comms. April, May 1974, p. 300.

Chapter 4

1. 42 U.S.C. Sec. 2162 authorizes the Atomic Energy Commission (now the Nuclear Research Agency) to keep information secret; P.L. 86-36, May 29, 1959, authorizes the National Security Agency to keep secret its communications and cryptographic activity; 50 U.S.C. Sec. 403 authorizes the CIA to keep secret information respecting its organization structure and personnel. Supporting legislation for atomic secrecy

includes an elaborate classification system backed by criminal penalties and the threat of court injunctions against disclosure; see 42 U.S.C. Secs. 2271-81. Communications intelligence is also protected by specific criminal sanctions; see 18 U.S.C. Sec. 798.

2. For the complete text of Executive Order No. 11652 see 3 C. F.R. 344 (1974).

3. National Security Council Directive Governing the Classification, Downgrading, Declassification and Safeguarding of National Security Information, May 17, 1972, printed in *Federal Register,* Vol. 37, No. 98, May 19, 1972.

4. The House Committee on Government Information was able, with great difficulty, to obtain a very partial—if long—list of such indicators. Hearings on U.S. Government Information Policies and Practices—The Pentagon Papers, before a Subcommittee of the House Committee on Government Operations, 92d Congress, 1st Sess. (1971), Part 2.

5. War Powers Resolution, Public Law 93-148, 93d Congress, House Joint Resolution 542, November 7, 1973, 87 Stat. 555-560, printed in Legislation on Foreign Relations, House Committee on Foreign Affairs and Senate Committee on Foreign Relations, 93d Congress, 2d Sess., March 1974, p. 1113.

6. See *War Powers: A Test of Compliance,* Hearings before the House International Relations Committee, Subcomm. on International Security and Scientific Affairs, 94th Cong, 1st Sess., May 7 to June 4, 1975.

7. The "Nelson" Amendment to the Foreign Assistance Act of 1973 (S. 1743), cited in Legislation on Foreign Relations, Senate Committee on Foreign Relations, June 1975, 94th Cong., 1st Sess., 1975, p. 240.

8. P.L. 94-329, 94th Cong., June 30, 1976, 90 Stat 729, amending 22 U.S.C. Sec. 2761.

9. On the Spanish agreement see Hearing on Spain and Portugal, before the Subcommittee on U.S Security Agreements and Commitments Abroad, Senate Committtee on Foreign Relations, 91st Congress, 2d Sess. (1969-1970), pp. 2356-2357. The text of Nixon's letter to Thieu was reprinted in the *New York Times,* May 1, 1975, p. 16.

10. Public Law 92-403, S. 596, Aug. 22, 1972.

11. 410 U.S. 73 (1973).

12. U.S. Government Information Policies and Practices—The Pentagon Papers, Hearings, subcommittee of the House Committee on Government Operations, 92d Congress, 1st Sess., Parts 1-3, 8, 9, 1971.

Executive Privilege, Secrecy in Government, Freedom of Information, Hearings, Subcommittees of the Senate Committee on Government Operations and the Senate Committee on the Judiciary, 93d Congress, 1st Sess. , Vol. 1-3, 1973.

Security Classification Reform, Hearings, Subcommittee of the House Committee on Government Operations, 93d Cong, 2nd Sess., 1974.

13. See Freedom of Information Act and Amendments of 1974 (P.L. 93-502); Source Book: Legislative History, Texts and other Documents, House Committee on Government Operations and Senate Committee on the Judiciary, 94th Cong., 1st Sess., March 1975, p. 217. Hereafter referred to as "Source Book."

14. In 1976 Congress revised exemption (b)(3), relating to statutes authorizing information to be kept secret. See generally Christine M. Marwick (ed.) *Litigation Under the Amended Federal Freedom of Information Act* (Washington, D.C.: Project on National Security and Civil Liberties, 1976).

15. This standard is drawn from Executive Order 11652, and the implementing NSC

directive of May 19, 1972. Read literally, the Executive Order seems to suggest that the appropriateness of authorizing the disclosure hinges on an assessment of the consequences of *un*authorized disclosure. We do not believe that such an illogical interpretation was intended, nor does it appear to represent existing practice. If authorized disclosure would cause no harm, it should be granted.

16. Source Book pp. 226, 229.

17. See Weekly Compilation of Presidential Documents, Vol. 10. No. 42, October 17, 1974.

18. We discuss the legal arguments further in Chapter 6. The House debate, Nov. 20, 1974, and the Senate debate, Nov. 21, 1974, are reprinted in the Source Book, pp. 403-480.

19. See Abstracts of Foreign Policy and National Defense Documents released under the Freedom of Infomation Act, (Washington, D.C).: Project on National Security and Civil Liberties, Nov., 1976.

20. See first footnote of this chapter.

21. 50 U.S.C. sections 403 (D) (3) and 403 (g)

22. *Phillippi* v. *CIA*, No. 76-1004,546 F. 2d 1009 (D.C. Cir. Nov. 16, 1976).

23. See generally, Christine M. Marwick, "The Freedom of Information Act and National Security Secrecy: How It's Working After Two Years," *First Principles,* Vol. II, No. 4, December 1976.

24. For the text of various bills and hearings on them, see "Security Classification Reform" Hearings before a Subcommittee of the Committee on Government Operations, House of Representatives, 93d Cong., 2d Sess. on H.R. 12004 (1974) and "Government Secrecy" Hearings before the Subcommittee on Intergovermental Relations of the Senate Committee on Government Operations, 93d Cong., 2d Sess., on S.1520, S.1726, S.2451, S.2738, S.3393 and S.3399 (1974). The texts of the Senate bills are collected in "Legislation on Government" committee print of the Subcommittee on Intergovernmental Relations (1974).

25. Executive Order 11652, Sec. 5(b)(3).

26. See, for example, the response of the State Department's Director of Politico-Military Affairs to a request under the Freedom of Information Act. This official had classified certain information "confidential," he explained in a letter, because its release "could cause injury." Further inquiry revealed that he had never heard the phrase "could reasonably be expected to cause injury," had not read the new executive order, and was not aware of the fact that the definition of confidential had changed. See *Halperin* v. *Secretary of State,* Civil Action # 75-0674, D.C. District Court, deposition of George Vest.

Chapter 5

1. For a careful review of the modern experience, see David Wise, *The Politics of Lying* (New York: Random House, 1973)

2. The first proposal for an automatic release category was made by Stanley Futterman. See Futterman, "What Is the Real Problem with the Classification System," in Norman Dorsen and Stephen Gillers, *None of Your Business* (New York: Viking, 1974), pp. 93-104. See also Brief of the American Civil Liberties Union, Amicus Curiae, *New York Times Co.* v. *U.S.,* 403 U.S. 713 (1971), reprinted in *U.S. Government Information Policies and Practices—The Pentagon Papers*(Part 3), U.S. Government Printing Office, 1971.

3. The question of what techniques Congress might use to guard against leaks of this information by its members and staff needs comment, for the record of congressional leaks has, of course, reinforced presidential reluctance to supply secret information to Congress. Our answer is that our system would give few occasions for Congress to handle information secretly. Most of this information is already protected by the laws described in Chapter 4. See note one and accompanying text. Moreover, this kind of information has seldom been the subject of leaks in the past and will not be likely to leak from Congress unless it is in fact more political than technical in character. The area of potential difficulty is therefore narrow, and we think it does not lend itself to a legislated solution. Under Article I, section 5 of the Cosntitution, Congress has an independent, internal discretion in the matter of secrecy. Moreover, members who reveal information would seem protected by the immunity of Article I, section 6. Thus we offer no legislative proposals concerning congressional secrecy.

4. We shall not attempt to confront here the technical aspects of drafting legislation that avoids undesired loopholes. For a draft bill that incorporates much but not all of our proposal see H.R. 15353, 94th Cong., 2d Sess.

5. Proliferation of Nuclear Weapons, Hearing, Subcommittee of the Joint Committee on Atomic Energy, 93d Cong., 2d Sess., Sept. 10, 1974, M14, 17, 24.

6. P.L. 94-329, 94th Cong. June 30, 1976. 90 Stat 729, amending 22 U.S.C. Sec. 2761.

7. Public Law 92-403, S.596, August 22, 1972.

8. Report of the Special Committee to Study Questions Related to Secret and Confidential Documents, 93d Cong., 1st Sess., Oct. 12, 1973, Report No. 93-466.

9. Nomination of William E. Colby, Hearing, Committee on Armed Services, United States Senate, 93d Cong. 1st Sess. 1973.

10. See Legislative History of the Central Intelligence Agency as Documented In Published Congressional Sources, Congressional Research Service (Library of Congress), UB 250 USA, 75-5A, 558/114, Ed. Grover S. Williams, January 8, 1975.

11. This is a subject of considerable debate in the scientific community; see for example the Seitz Report, *op. cit.* at n. 15 below.

12. PL 93-559, Dec. 30, 1974.

13. The subject of specific congressional secrecy and disclosure procedures is beyond the scope of this study; see footnote 3 above.

14. This list draws from two sources: the ACLU brief in the Pentagon Papers civil suit (see n. 2) and the Seitz Report (see n. 15). The Seitz committee reached the conclusion that a policy of no secrecy would be most desirable; since that was not politically feasible, they recommended that secrecy be limited to a few categories.

15. There is a contrary argument, supported by many scientists, to the effect that keeping such information secret hinders American research even more than it handicaps potential adversaries. For example, soon after World War II, the United States made the decision to declassify most computer technology information. The substantial and continuing American lead in computer technology may not have occurred if all such technology had been kept secret. See, for example, the testimony of Edward Teller, printed in *Legislative Proposals to Strengthen Congressional Oversight of the Nation's Intelligence Agencies*, Hearings, Subcommittee on Intergovernmental Relations of the Senate Committee on Government Operations, 93rd Cong., 2nd Sess. 1974; and the *Seitz Report* on Security Classification Reform, Hearings, Subcommittee of the House Committee on Government Operations, 93rd Cong., 2nd Sess. 1974, p. 623.

16. Affidavit of Jeane W. Davis, July 25, 1975, in *Halperin v. National Security Council*, No. 75-0675, District Court, District of Columbia. Ms. Davis later added

that "The publication of the decision making process of the President in the area of foreign policy would have an adverse effect upon the President's ability to act effectively in the area of foreign policy and is thus prohibited by the preamble of Executive Order 11652 and Section 1 of the Order." Response to Interrogatories, October 20, 1975.

17. Some documents may contain both matter requiring disclosure and matter that is properly kept secret, perhaps for reasons of "privilege" unrelated specifically to their national security content; for example, advice to a superior, or information about an individual's private life. In such a case the privileged matter should be segregated and exempted from disclosure; the Freedom of Information Act already contains provision for such treatment.

18. The current state of the law of espionage and of prior restraint is discussed in appendices to this study, and the Freedom of Information Act was introduced in Chapter 4.

19. In that event, the (b)(3) exemption relating to information authorized by legislation to be kept secret would be redundant as far as national security information is concerned.

20. Constitutional objections to the Freedom of Information Act are discussed in the next chapter.

21. See, for example, Meiklejohn, *The First Amendment Is An Absolute,* 1961 Supreme Court Review, p. 245.

22. This is a paraphrase of Mr. Justice Stewart's opinion, now generally cited as reflecting the view of a majority of the court. See Appendix B for a detailed analysis of the various opinions and the overall result of the decision.

23. See Appendix B for detailed analysis of this very complex litigation.

24. See Appendix A for a detailed treatment of these laws and the legal issues they raise.

25. One known indictment under 18 U.S.C. Sec. 798 resulted in a guilty plea; see the *Washington Post,* Jan. 5, 1955.

26. 403 U.S. 713, 729 (1971) (concurring opinion).

Chapter 6

1. At the Virginia ratifying convention; see 3 Farrand, *Proceedings of the Federal Convention,* at 233.

2. Article II, Sections 2 and 3.

3. Article I, Section 8, paragraphs 11 through 16.

4. See 1 Farrand, *Ibid.,* at 65-74, 112, 140, 144.

5. See 2 Farrand, *Ibid.,* at 538-49.

6. A full-length study of secrecy in the Federalist period is being prepared by one of the authors of this book, Daniel Hoffman.

7. For further discussion of the judicial role in interbranch secrecy disputes, see R. Berger, *Executive Privilege,* (Cambridge: Harvard University Press, 1974), Ch. 11.

8. The same conclusion is ably developed by Prof. D. Frohnmeyer in "An Essay on Executive Privilege," printed in the *Congressional Record,* April 30, 1974, at Page S6603.

9. See generally, Edwin S. Corwin, *The President: Office and Powers, 1787-1957,* 4th rev. ed. (New York: New York University Press), pp. 227-262.

10. See *ibid.,* pp. 170-226.

11. The applicability of the Bill of Rights and other constitutional limitations to national security powers is confirmed by such cases as *Hamilton* v. *Kentucky Distilleries & Warehouse Co.,* 251 U.S. 146 (1919); *Home Building & Loan Association* v. *Blaisdell,* 290 U.S. 398 (1934); *Kennedy* v. *Mendoza-Martinez,* 372 U.S. 144 (1963); and *United States* v. *Robel,* 389 U.S. 258 (1967).

12. *U.S.* v. *Klein,* 13 Wall. 128 (1871); *Myers* v. *U.S.,* 272 U.S. 52 (1926).

13. The leading modern case in point is the *Steel Seizure* case, *Youngstown Sheet & Tube Co.* v. *Sawyer,* 343 U.S. 579 (1952); see especially the very incisive concurring opinion of Mr. Justice Jackson.

14. *In re Debs,* 158 U.S. 554 (1895); *Oetjen* v. *Central Leather Co.,* 264 U.S. 297 Z1918); *U.S.* v. *Curtis-Wright Export Corp.,* 299 U.S. 304 (1936); *U.S.* v. *Belmont,* 301 U.S. 324 (1937); *U.S.* v. *Pink,* 315 U.S. 203 (1942); *Hirabavashi* v. *U.S..,* 320 U.S. 81 (1942); and *Cafeteria Workers* v. *McElroy,* 367 U.S. 886 (1961).

15. Corwin, *op. cit.,* p. 177. See also *Baker* v. *Carr,* 369 U.S. 186 (1962) for the most thorough modern judicial treatment of the "political questions doctrine."

16. *U.S.* v. *U.S. District Court,* 408 U.S. 297, 320 (1972).

17. See *Marbury* v. *Madison,* 5 U.S. (1 Cranch) 137 (1803); *U.S.* v. *Burr,* 25 Fed. Cas. 30, 55, 187 (Cir. Ct. Va. 1807); *Totten* v. *U.S.,* 92 U.S. 105 (1876); *Chicago & Southern Airlines* v. *Waterman Steamship Co.,* 333 U.S. 103 (1948); *U.S.* v. *Reynolds,* 345 U.S. 1 (1953); *EPA* v. *Mink,* 410 U.S. 73 (1973); and *U.S.* v. *Nixon,* 418 U.S. 683 (1974).

18. A very similar approach, inviting Congress to provide for judicial review of deportation decisions, was taken in *Knauff* v. *Shaughnessy,* 338 U.S. 537 (1950).

19. Hearings on S.2224, Senate Comm. on Foreign Relations, 92d Cong., 2d Sess. (1972), Taken from Schwartzman, Fiscal Oversight of the CIA, 7 N.T.U. *Journal of International Law and Politics* 493, 516 n. 96 (1974).

20. Leslie Gelb, "House Votes Missile Site Planned for 6 Months' Use," *New York Times,* August 8, 1974, p. 1.

21. Report to the Secretary of Defense by the (Coolidge) Committee on Classified Information, Nov. 8, 1956, in House Government Operations Committee Hearings on Availability of Information from Federal Departments and Agencies, Part 7, p. 2134, 84th Cong., 1957; Report of (Wright) Commission on Government Security pursuant to P.L. 304, 84th Cong., 1957; report of the (Seitz) Defense Science Board Task Force on Secrecy, July 1970, in Hearings, Subcommittee of the House Government Operations Committee, 93d Cong., 2d Sess., 1974, p. 623; Report of the (Murphy) Commission on the Organization of the Government for the Conduct of Foreign Policy, June 1975.

Chapter 7

1. Morton H. Halperin, Jerry J. Berman, Robert L. Borosage and Christine M. Marwick, *The Lawless State: The Crimes of The U.S. Intelligence Agencies* (New York: Penguin Books, 1976).

2. S. K. Padover, *The Complete Madison,* at p. 337.

Appendix A

1. For an exhaustive analysis of the espionage laws in relation to the publication of information, see Harold Edgar and Benno C. Schmidt, Jr., *The Espionage Statutes and the Publication of Defense Information,* 73 *Columbia Law Review* 930-1087

(May 1973). Our discussion draws heavily on their analysis, which covers the origins and meaning of the law as it developed prior to the indictment of Ellsberg and Russo.

2. See, e.g., *Aptheker* v. *Secretary of State*, 378 U.S. 500 (1954); *U.S.* v. *Robel*, 389 U.S. 258 (1967).

3. See, e.g., *Musser* v. *Utah*, 333 U.S. 95 (1948); *Baggett* v. *Bullitt*, 377 U.S. 360 (1964).

4. See title 18 U.S. Code sections 793-798 and 952; 50 U.S.C. Appendix section 781; and 42 U.S.C. sections 2271-81.

5. See M.C. Miskovsky, *The Espionage Laws*, Office of General Counsel Monograph, CIA, 1961; Statement of Abram Chayes (Witness #8), former Legal Advisor, Department of Defense, at p. 21 of Affidavit of Goodell & Nesson, June 7, 1972, in support of Motion To Dismiss for Selective Prosecution, *United States* v. *Russo & Ellsberg,* No. 9373-WMB-CD (C.D. Cal. 1972); Brief for Petitioner at 52-53, *New York Times Co.* v. *United States,* 403 U. S. 713 (1971) and House of Representatives Report No. 1895, 81st Cong. 2d Sess. (1950).

6. A further obstacle to indictment may have been the need to disclose the content and significance of the information, in order to persuade the jury that the information truly related to the national defense. This block against indictments has become particularly important in the post-Pentagon Papers era, when other restraints appear to have lost much of their potency.

7. House of Representatives Report No. 1895, "Enhancing Further the Security of the United States by Preventing Disclosures of Information Concerning the Cryptographic Systems and the Communication Intelligence Activities of the United States," 81st Cong., 2d Sess. (1950).

8. See, for example, *Hearings on Strategic Arms Limitation Agreements* before the Senate Foreign Relations Committee, 92d Cong., 2d Sess. (July, 1972); and *Hearings on Tactical Nuclear Weapons in Europe* before the Subcommittee on Commitments of the Senate Foreign Relations Committee, 93d Cong., 2d Sess. (1975). The Foreign Relations committees of both houses, the Government Operations committees, and the Joint Economic Committee have ardently sought information obtained by former officials during their government employment.

9. *Op. cit.,* n. 7.

10. See *Report on Executive Classification of Information—Security Classification Problems Involving Exemption (b) (1) of the Freedom of Information Act (5 U.S.C. 552),* House Committee on Government Operations, 93d Cong., 1st Sess. (1973); *Hearings on United States Government Information Policies and Practices—The Pentagon Papers,* before a Subcommittee of the House Committee on Government Operations, 92d Cong., 1st and 2d Sess. (1971-1972) (9 volumes); and *Hearings on Executive Privilege, Secrecy in Government, and Freedom of Information,* before the Subcommittee on Intergovernmental Relations of the Senate Committee on Government Operations and the Subcommittees on Separation of Powers and Administrative Practice and Procedure of the Senate Committee on the Judiciary, 93d Cong., 1st Sess. (1973) (3 volumes).

11. *Gorin* v. *United States,* 312 U.S. 19, 28 (1941).

12. *United States* v. *Heine,* 151 F.2d 813, 814-15 (2d Cir. 1945), *cert. denied,* 328 U.S. 833 (1946).

13. *Gorin* v. *United States, supra,* 312 U.S. at 28.

14. 151 F.2d at 816.

15. 50 U.S.C. Sec. 783(b).

16. *United States* v. *Scarbeck*, 317F.2d 546 (D.C. Cir. 1962), *cert. denied*, 374 U.S. 856 (1963).

17. *United States* v. *Drummond*, 354F.2d 132 (2d Cir. 1965), *cert. denied*, 384 U.S. 1013 (1966).

18. The text of Byrne's oral opinion is reprinted in the House Judiciary Committee Impeachment Inquiry: *Hearings on House Resolution 803, Statement of Information*, 93d Cong., 2d Sess., Book VII, part 4, at 2076 (1974). The only aspects of the Pentagon Papers criminal trial to be officially reported were decisions involving a wiretapping of one of the lawyers in the case. See *Russo* v. *Byrne*, 409 U.S. 1013(1972) (*cert. denied*, Douglas, J., dissenting); 409 U.S. 1219 (1972) (stay granted per Douglas, J.). A full set of the formal files and transcripts of the Pentagon Papers criminal trial is on file at the Harvard Law School Library.

19. Ellsberg was also charged with one count under 793(c): obtaining documents related to the national defense with the intent to use them in violation of section (d) or (e). Both defendants, in addition, were charged with theft of government property, conspiracy to commit espionage, and conspiracy to defraud the United States, raising technical issues not considered here.

20. Lynda Sinay, the owner of the advertising agency whose xerox machine was used for the copying, and Vu Van Thai, a Vietnamese diplomat and former ambassador to the United States, were named as unindicted co-conspirators; it was alleged that one or more volumes of the study had been "transferred" to Sinay and Thai as well as to Russo in that they helped to xerox those volumes.

21. The indictment is printed as an appendix in Peter Schrag, *Test of Loyalty* (New York: Simon & Schuster, 1974).

22. Compare *United States* v. *Drummond*, 354F.2d 132 (2d Cir. 1965), *cert. denied*, 384 U.S. 1013 (1966), approving jury instructions to the effect that "Whether any given document relates to the national defense is a question of fact for you to decide. It is not a question of how they were marked."

23. Trial transcript, 8219 to 8220.

24. See P. Schrag, *Test of Loyalty* (New York: Simon & Schuster, 1974), pp. 361-64.

25. The Court of Appeals in *Gorin* had remarked that a serious problem would have arisen had the defendants alleged that *all* the information listed in the indictment was available from public sources. *Gorin* v. *United States*, 111 F. 2d 712, at 722 (9th Cir. 1940).

26. This issue came up as well in the *Marchetti* prior restraint case, where the court reached a very different conclusion. See the discussion in Appendix B.

27. The Industrial Security Manual is issued by the Defense Department and applies to defense industry generally; the Rand manual pertains to that organization only. The Industrial Security Manual is printed in the *Security and Loyalty Reporter*, published by the Bureau of National Affairs, at 25:10-1.

28. Edgar and Schmidt, *supra,* 73 *Columbia Law Review* at 1051-52.

29. Transcript, at 12, 171 ff.

30. Transcript, at p. 8221. Here, of course, the court was quoting from the definition of "confidential" in Executive Order 10501. A document is classifiable only if it could be said to meet this minimum standard.

Appendix B

1. See, for example, *United States* v. *U.S. District Court*, 407 U.S. 297 (1972), in which the Court declined to accept the executive branch's determination that there was a need for warrantless domestic electronic surveillance; and *Lamont* v. *Postmaster General*, 381 U.S. 301 (1965), in which the Court struck down a law requiring citizens to file a written request before they could receive communist propaganda through the mails.

2. The government's brief to the Supreme Court, and other briefs, orders, and opinions cited below, are reprinted in *The New York Times Company* v. *United States, A Documentary History*, 2 vols., (New York: Arno Press, 1971). The Supreme Court decision is reported officially at 403 U.S. 713 (1971).

3. The three precedents cited had to do with publications allegedly obscene, libelous, and invasive of individual privacy, respectively. The *per curiam* opinion did not note that the motivation for speech was different in each case, ranging from the mainly commercial to political advocacy and information. However, it seems clear that if the government could once show a regulatory interest sufficiently compelling to pass the threshhold presumption against prior restraint, the strength of the specific, competing speech interest would become a critical issue.

4. For one statement of the argument that the First Amendment was intended to ban absolutely all interferences with publication, see Meiklejon, "The First Amendment Is an Absolute," 1961 *Supreme Court Review*, p. 245.

5. Except in the special case of atomic energy secrets. Atomic Energy Act, 42 U.S.C. section 2280.

6. See p. 135.

7. In order to decide the merits of these cases properly, some or all of the following questions should have been faced:

Whether the Attorney General is authorized to bring these suits in the name of the United States. Compare *In re Debs*, 158 U.S. 564 (1895), with *Youngstown Sheet & Tube Co.* v. *Sawyer*, 343 U.S. 579 (1952). This question involves as well the construction and validity of a singularly opaque statute—the Espionage Act, 18 U.S.C. § 793 (e).

Whether the First Amendment permits the federal courts to enjoin publication of stories which would present a serious threat to national security. See *Near* v. *Minnesota*, 283 U.S. 697, 716 (1931) (dictum).

Whether the threat to publish highly secret documents is of itself a sufficient implication of national security to justify an injunction on the theory that regardless of the contents of the documents harm enough results simply from the demonstration of such a breach of secrecy.

Whether the unauthorized disclosure of any of these particular documents would seriously impair the national security.

What weight should be given to the opinion of high officers in the Executive Branch of the Government with respect to questions 3 and 4.

Whether the newspapers are entitled to retain and use the documents notwithstanding the seemingly uncontested facts that the documents, or the originals of which they are duplicates, were purloined from the Government's possession and that the newspapers received them with knowledge that they had been feloniously acquired. Cf. *Liberty Lobby, Inc.* v. *Pearson*, 390 F. 2d 489 (CADC 1968).

Whether the threatened harm to the national security or the Government's possessory interest in the documents justifies the issuance of an injunction against publication in light of—
The strong First Amendment policy against prior restraints on publication;
The doctrine against enjoining conduct in violation of criminal statutes; and
The extent to which the materials at issue have apparently already been otherwise disseminated.

8. That the *New York Times* decision turned fundamentally on the question of separation of powers is also the conclusion of Junker, "Down Memory Lane: The Case of the Pentagon Papers," 23 *Case W. Res. L. Rev.* 3 (1971).

9. The litigation originated as *United States* v. *Marchetti,* No. 179-71-A (E.D.Va. 1972), *injunction affirmed,* 466 F.2d 1309 (4th Cir. 1972), *cert. denied,* 409 U.S. 1063 (1972) (three Justices dissenting). The subsequent proceedings are styled *Knopf, Inc.* v. *Colby,* No. 540-73-A (E.D.Va. 1974), *affirmed in part and vacated in part,* 509 F.2d 1362 (4th Cir. 1975), *cert. denied,* 421 U.S. 992 (1975), *order issued,* Oct. 22, 1975 (E.D. Va.).

10. 50 U.S.C. section 403(d)(3).

11. 466 F.2d at 1315.

12. See Chapter 4.

13. 509 F.2d at 1367.

14. The court did not dispute the district judge's finding that procedural requirements had not in fact been observed; nor did they discuss the significance of the Conference Report to the Freedom of Information Act, where it is specified that both substantive and procedural errors in classification will remove a document from the protection of the (b)(1) exemption.

15. See Victor Marchetti and John D. Marks, *The CIA and the Cult of Intelligence* (New York: Knopf, 1974). See also Marks, "On Being Censored," *Foreign Policy,* Summer 1974, p. 93.

16. It can also be argued that the court failed to apply correctly the principles of contract law itself. The burden on Marchetti of a permanent censorship over both fiction and nonfiction writing on intelligence seems quite harsh. Private employers are not usually entitled to injunctive enforcement of such contractual terms as will prevent ex-employees from pursuing their professions. Yet the district court justified its injunction simply by noting the inadequacy of monetary damages to compensate the government for its loss. The appropriateness of this one-sided test was not discussed by the Fourth Circuit.

17. 50 U.S.C. Secs. 403 (d)(3) and 403 (g).

18. 360 U.S. 474 (1959).

19. *Youngstown Sheet and Tube Company* v. *Sawyer,* 343 U.S. 579, 635-37 (1952).

20. See Edgar and Schmidt, "The Espionage Statutes and the Publication of Defense Information," 73 *Columbia Law Review* 930, 952 (May 1973).

21. *Ibid,* at 1027.

22. Atomic Energy Act, 42 U.S.C. section 2280.

23. An early version of such a proposal was part of the record in *Marchetti.* In February 1976 President Ford actually submitted to Congress proposed legislation that would permit the courts to enjoin the publication of information revealing intelligence sources and methods. This proposal was not seriously considered and no hearings were held.

24. See Appendix A.

25. Griswold, "Teaching Alone Is Not Enough," 25 *J. Legal Ed.* 251, 257 (1973).

Index

153

Composed in Times Roman by New Republic Books, Washington, D.C.

Printed and bound by BookCrafters, Inc., Fredericksburg, Virginia.

Designed by Gerard Valerio